in Dallas

Hugh C. McDonald
As told to
Geoffrey Bocca

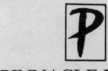

PINNACLE BOOKS
Kensington Publishing Corp.
http://www.kensingtonbooks.com

PINNACLE BOOKS are published by

Kensington Publishing Corp.
119 West 40th Street
New York, NY 10018

All Kensington Titles, Imprints, and Distributed Lines are available at special quantity discounts for bulk purchases for sales promotions, premiums, fund-raising, and educational or institutional use. Special book excerpts or customized printings can also be created to fit specific needs. For details, write or phone the office of the Kensington special sales manager: Kensington Publishing Corp., 119 West 40th Street, New York, NY 10018, attn: Special Sales Department, Phone: 1-800-221-2647.

Pinnacle and the P logo Reg. U.S. Pat. & TM Off.

ISBN-13: 978-0-7860-3315-7
ISBN-10: 0-7860-3315-0
First Kensington Mass Market Edition: 1975

ISBN-13: 978-0-7860-3316-4
ISBN-10: 0-7860-3316-9
First Kensington Electronic Edition: October 2013

10 9 8 7 6 5 4 3 2

Printed in the United States of America

In June, 1975, a reputable literary agent introduced Zebra Books to a man and a story. The story was hard to believe; the man was not.

Hugh C. McDonald was a veteran law enforcement officer who supplied credentials which, to us, were outstanding.

We are aware that APPOINTMENT IN DALLAS is a controversial book. The story Hugh McDonald tells adds further doubt to the already questioned Warren Commission Report. There will be those who will try to smear McDonald's story. And perhaps if this story was told by a man with credentials other than those of Hugh McDonald, it would be inconceivable.

Kensington is publishing APPOINTMENT IN DALLAS because we believe no one has the right to hold back a shred of information that might possibly throw even the faintest light on one of the darkest moments in our history.

The Publishers

In the Intelligence Community, as well as the newspaper business, sources of information must remain inviolate. Therefore certain names, dates, places and events in this book have been altered or disguised to protect people whose lives might be endangered.

The facts of Saul's confession are just as they were told to me in the Westbury Hotel in London, England. Any literary coloration is at the behest of my co-author.

Hugh C. McDonald

FOREWORD

Of all the questions that have been asked regarding Saul's admission and the circumstances leading up to his conversation with me, the one that seems to be most pertinent refers to the reason why I held this information literally to myself from 1972 until 1975.

It is a good and fair question—and demands a reasonable answer.

It was in July, 1972 that I returned from that trip which had finally brought me together with Saul. At that point I had confirmation only of the fact that Herman Kimsey told me the truth in Dallas, eight years before. Saul said that he talked to Herman and that he told him the story Herman related to me. I was glad. I respected Herman Kimsey. In many ways he was a great man. I have the feeling his full story will never be told. I feel glad that this ideal had not been shattered.

I had no proof *per se* of the truth of Saul's statement. He could have lied originally to Herman, and nine years later carried on that lie with me. I wanted to be as sure, as positive, as was humanly possible of Saul's story as I now was of Herman's. This would take time. I had to check the statement against the facts and I decided to use the Warren Commission Report as my source of those facts.

The result is contained in the pages of APPOINT-MENT IN DALLAS.

There did come a time when I was convinced that proof of Saul's statement was existing and available. Now my dilemma was what to do with Herman's and Saul's statements, both given to me, and the proof of those statements. All of my adult life I had been an "Establishment Man." I feel that I still am.

It would have been most natural for me to have taken the information to my colleagues in the Central Intelligence Agency or the Federal Bureau of Investigation. Circumstances existing at that time prevented me from going this route.

First, let us consider the CIA. I knew them and respected them, but something was wrong. If I took the story to them, it would be like bringing coal to Newcastle. They knew of Saul. I first met him in their headquarters. They took the picture of him that started my investigation. But, under oath, the deputy director of that agency, who later became the director, Richard Helms, testified that he did not know Saul. This inconsistency warned me that if the information I had came into the hands of that agency, it could be buried, classified, and the American people would never hear it.

What about the FBI? I was even closer to them. On the date of my retirement, their director, John Edgar Hoover, had sent a warm, congratulatory wire from Washington, D.C. I had, and believe I still have, close personal friends who are members of that agency. The FBI is, in my opinion, the finest investigative body in the world; but it is a governmental agency, and as such, is—as was being demonstrated exactly at the time of my decision (i.e. at the time of Watergate)—subject to serious political pressures. Saul's story was so explosive that it could have serious political ramifications. I decided that the FBI was not the place to take that story.

Where, then?

Watergate probably led the way. Where was the one forum that would hear the story, evaluate it against the known facts, and render a fair verdict regardless of political and/or other pressures? The American press, and through them, to the American people. No holds barred, tell it the way it happened.

Once that decision was made, I had to be careful in selecting the proper contact into the media. All kinds of people had theories about the assassination: sincere people, honest people, and kooks. Saul's story must not get enmeshed with any of these.

I took the story to New York.

Two publishers offered to print the story. But they would not do it as a documentary. They were afraid of interference from official agencies. They would print the story only if it were fictionalized and made no claim to truth. This I refused to do.

In June of 1975, I was introduced to Zebra Books. They recognized the many obstacles, but they decided to go forward.

And now the American people are going to read APPOINTMENT IN DALLAS.

ABOUT THE AUTHOR

One of the reasons Hugh C. McDonald is not better known to the world today is that on May 3, 1960, he did not fly a U2 over the Soviet Union. He was offered the job, and he refused. He was asked why. He replied, "The money is good, but the risk is too great."

His CIA colleagues were derisive. U2s had been flying over Russia on photo reconnaissance for four years, since the ever-suspicious Russians rejected an "open skies" proposal of the United States. The Russians did not have the weapons to shoot them down. They did not even know of their existence.

McDonald held his views firm. "If that's what you believe, fine. Get someone else to do it."

The CIA decided that poor old Hugh, then forty-seven years old, was prematurely chicken.

And so on May 3rd, the United States cautiously issued a story that a U2 engaged in "meteorological duty" may have been forced down inside the Soviet border due to mechanical failure. Two days later the Russians announced that it had been shot down twelve hundred miles inside the Soviet Union. And thus, the pilot, Francis Gary Powers, entered the history books instead of Hugh Chisholm McDonald.

Hugh McDonald was born in 1913, and his exploits as a policeman, private investigator, flier and intelligence agent are legendary in the closed and guarded world of the international espionage and counter-espionage service. He once deliberately crashed a small plane into the Black Sea behind the Iron Curtain as part of a mission successfully carried off.

These incidents, and many others, took place over a period of almost thirty years, while Hugh McDonald was a member of the Los Angeles County Sheriff's Department. He was frequently granted leave to be of service to several Government agencies.

When he retired, he held the post of Division Chief in the fifth largest law enforcement agency in the United States. He holds patents on the Identi-Kit and the Identicator, criminal identification systems used by police all over the world.

McDonald has taught at the University of California at Los Angeles, the University of Southern California, the University of Oklahoma and the University of Louisville, Kentucky. He is a graduate of the sixty-seventh class of the Federal Bureau of Investigation Academy in Washington, D.C. His books, *The Investigation of Sex Crimes, The Classification of Police Photographs* and *The Psychology of Police Interrogation,* are standard texts in most Police Academies.

A partial resume of his activities follows:

February 1967—Retired as Chief of Detectives, Los Angeles County Sheriff's Department, in direct control and command of some six hundred detective sergeants.

1963—Division Chief, Los Angeles County Sheriff's Department, commanding the Civil Division. This Division consists of approximately five hundred men and services the Superior Court System of the County of Los Angeles, which is the largest System in the world. This Division provides security for the Court System and handles all orders emanating from the Court System.

1958—Inspector, Los Angeles County Sheriff's Department, commanding a geographical area of Los Angeles County which included the beach area of Malibu, the mountain areas of Altadena, Montrose, Newhall and the Antelope Valley.

1956—Captain, Los Angeles County Sheriff's Department. Assigned to the Patrol Division as a Captain in command of the Hollywood Station. This is the Station which has in its territory the famous Sunset Strip, and is a territory which presents sensitive and unusual problems.

1951—Lieutenant, Los Angeles County Sheriff's Department. Assigned to the Detective Bureau and handled all types of investigations; was for a period of time the Commander of that Section of the Bureau which handled all sex crimes.

1949—Sergeant, Los Angeles County Sheriff's Department. Assigned Detective Bureau, general assignment.

1946 to 1954—Second in command of largest Military Intelligence School in the nation, Ft. McArthur, California. At present, Major, Military Intelligence in Retired Reserve.

1942 to 1946—U.S. Army. Entered as Private; attended O.C.S.; discharged 1946 as a Major, Military Intelligence.

Special Assignments:

1951—When the California Crime Commission declared that law enforcement had broken down in the City of Burbank, was assigned as Chief of Police of that city for a period of ninety days to restore law and order.

1953—When law enforcement broke down in the City of Azusa, was assigned to that city as Chief of Police for a period of ninety days to restore law and order.

1954—Hughes Aircraft, Industrial Security

1964—Although not a Republican, was selected by the Republican National Committee to head the security for Presidential candidate, Senator Barry Goldwater.

1964-65—Chairman of Communications Coordination Committee, California Peace Officers' Association.

1965-66—Chairman of Electronic Data Processing Advisory Committee, California Peace Officers' Association.

I
Dallas, Texas
Midafternoon
September, 1964

On August 2, 1964, Hugh McDonald, Chief of Detectives of the County of Los Angeles Sheriff's Department, accepted responsibility for the life and safety of Senator Barry Goldwater of Arizona. Although not a Republican, McDonald was appointed head of security for the duration of Senator Goldwater's Presidential campaign against Lyndon Johnson.

McDonald was then 51 years old. Although he looked like a cop, with his straight back, broad shoulders, and piercing blue eyes in a craggy Scotch-Irish face, he was, in fact, highly unusual within the realm of his métier. Indeed, he was somewhat of a Renaissance man, master of many fields of human endeavor. He was an intellectual. He spoke German and Japanese. He was an inventor; he conceived, perfected and patented Identi-Kit. He lectured. He was the author of three standard police textbooks: on interrogation, photograph classification, and sex crimes.

He possessed a strong sense of humor; he laughed readily and often. He had killed in self-defense. He had a keen eye for what an earlier generation would have called a well-turned ankle.

One of McDonald's first acts on his appointment

by Barry Goldwater was to hire his former boss in the Central Intelligence Agency, Herman Kimsey, to assist him. This was an odd and historically important reversal of roles, because when McDonald was under contract to the CIA, it was Kimsey who gave the orders.

In late October, 1964, eleven months after the assassination of President John F. Kennedy, McDonald and Kimsey found themselves in Dealey Plaza, Dallas, Texas, where Senator Goldwater was to speak the next day. Both men sweltered in their seersucker suits under the pouring Texas sun.

Kimsey had urgently asked McDonald for a few minutes alone together, on the spot where Kennedy had been killed.

"We are here," McDonald said. "We are alone, and I am hotter than Hades. Now what?" McDonald's voice, quite high, gentle and silky, was at odds with his husky frame.

Kimsey said, "If it looks like our man Goldwater can get elected, then you have to face the fact that there is a good chance he can get assassinated, too."

Since this was a thought he lived with every hour of each day, McDonald said nothing as he waited for Kimsey to go on.

He recalls that he was suddenly struck with the significance of where they stood. The events of November 22, 1963, began to unreel in his mind as vividly as so many millions had seen them on television that tragic day.

To his right was the grassy knoll which was the subject of so much speculation and controversy. He could envision the Presidential cavalcade as it wound through the underpass, preceded by the motorcycles of the Dallas police, Secret Service-men on the running boards of the second Official car. The haunting face of Jacqueline Kennedy beside the President was as clear to McDonald at that moment as though he had actually been present. The sound of today's traffic became the throttled-down roar of the motorcycle escort. Once again, as on that fatal day, came tears to his eyes.

"The President was shot from the second floor of that building," Kimsey said.

McDonald was slow to come out of his reverie. He looked toward the Texas Book Depository Building, and the window where Lee Harvey Oswald had stood with his mail order rifle.

It was only then he realized that Herman Kimsey's outstretched arm was pointing toward quite a different building—at right angles to the Book Depository. "The County Records Building."

"Herman, what the hell are you trying to tell me!"

Kimsey's voice was unsteady. "I'm telling you that Kennedy was shot from *that* building—and not by Lee Oswald! I'm telling you because I owe it to you! I work for *you* now. And it's something you've got to know—if you are going to protect Goldwater from more of the same!"

McDonald took Kimsey's elbow and steered him toward a deep-set doorway out of the sun. "Either I heard you wrong, Herman, or the sun is baking your brains. Don't let this Goldwater business get you down. Remember what we said at the beginning: no imagination, no bullshit, keep everything in perspective."

The bright blue eyes narrowed. "Goddamn you, McDonald, you forget who brought you into this business. Now for once, keep that big Irish mouth shut and listen." Once again, Herman was the boss.

"You remember the man you met in my office right after the Bay of Pigs?"

"Do I remember! You're referring to that mean son of a bitch who told you off pretty good? The one you described as a top assassin?"

Kimsey took McDonald and pointed him at the County Records Building. "Now listen. That man shot and killed President John Kennedy from the second floor of that building. I have the whole story. He told it to me—and you damned well better believe it."

"You," McDonald said, "have got to be crazy, but you're going to tell me all of it, Herman. Every Goddamned word! We're going back to the hotel. Now!"

He couldn't know it, but that moment started Hugh McDonald on a chase that lasted three years and took him fifty thousand miles to ten different countries and cost over thirty thousand dollars —until at the end he sat face to face with the man who killed John F. Kennedy—and heard him tell it as it really happened.

II
Washington
8:45 A.M.
April 27, 1961

It all began three years earlier, during the tense aftermath of the Bay of Pigs fiasco. Hugh McDonald was fifteen minutes early when he signed the visitors' register and was pinned with his identification badge at the Central Intelligence Agency on Connecticut Avenue. The signature was itself unusual. McDonald usually entered without signing, discreetly.

This was not the calm, well-ordered CIA he was used to. The confusion was unsettling. Even the photograph of President Kennedy hung slightly askew behind the reception desk. The Bay of Pigs disaster was ten days old.

On April 17, fourteen hundred Cuban refugees, trained and equipped by the CIA, had made a D-Day style landing on the beaches of Las Villas Province. In the first hours of euphoria, all sorts of stories erupted from the media . . .

The Cuban army had laid down its arms and joined the invaders . . .

Fidel Castro had flown out of the country, on his way to Moscow in the private jet he always kept ready for such an emergency . . .

The people of Havana were overflowing into the streets of the capital to welcome their liberators, who were less than fifty kilometres away. . . .

The bubble was quickly pricked. The insurgents were cut off, isolated by Castro's tanks and slaughtered by his jet interceptors. Their supply ships were sunk. They panicked, fled, and within three days it was all over. Fourteen hundred embittered Cuban refugees, trained, paid and equipped by the CIA, shuffled in lines to prisoner-of-war camps. Only a handful escaped, either into the jungle or out to sea.

The United States reeled in shock and outrage. The humiliation of the CIA was bitter. The world's most prestigious intelligence agency, which had always looked down its Ivy League nose at the carnival shenanigans of others, had committed the unforgivable blunder—had insisted on punitive action based on its own information, information which was hopelessly wrong—and fatal.

McDonald, ordinarily a fashionable dresser, always wore an inconspicuous dark blue suit and a white shirt when visiting the CIA. He crossed the lobby unobtrusively and took the elevator to the second floor. He knocked on the door of his friend, Herman Kimsey, and entered quietly. Kimsey was talking on the telephone, in a low, tense voice, crouched so that for a mad moment McDonald thought he was talking to someone lying on the ground behind the desk. Kimsey glanced up, waved McDonald to a chair, and went on talking.

McDonald looked around him. The office was small and meagerly furnished. The desk was adequate but worn, ringed with coffee stains. He noted that it was currently adorned with a glass of water and a bottle of indigestion tablets. The floor was carpetless, covered in nondescript asphalt tile. The only decoration was a small ceramic bear painted with the number of Kimsey's old military CIC unit from World War II. Behind him stood a bookcase filled with technical books and law manuals.

Kimsey hung up, twirled in his swivel chair, shook hands across the desk, and said, "Sorry, Hugh, I couldn't get you in time to cancel your visit. All hell is breaking loose here. In a few minutes we have a debriefing session with some of the people who got out, so I'll have to run soon. What brings you in from the Coast?"

McDonald was truly sympathetic. He had known, as soon as he read the initial reports of the invasion, that Kimsey had to be involved. Cuba was his territory. That was the reason for McDonald's visit. He said, diffidently, "I'm attending the FBI National Academy . . ." But he could see Kimsey was less than interested, so he came to the point. "Errand of mercy, Herman. I hope you can help. I know Sandy Henderson was training the attack force in Guatemala. Can you tell me anything more, in confidence? Did he hit the beach?"

Kimsey looked around him, a strange act in itself. McDonald could not conceive that the CIA would actually bug its own headquarters. Kimsey held both wrists up in front of him, and, in pantomime, tried to pull them apart, as though they were tied or handcuffed together. McDonald's heart sank for Sandy Henderson. He knew his friend was a prisoner of Castro.

Kimsey had given McDonald his first contract assignment, and every assignment afterwards originated with Kimsey. Kimsey was a hard, unemotional man from who-knows-where, and McDonald had never seen him look agitated before.

"What are his chances?"

As McDonald waited for a reply, a man burst into the room with such violence that the windows rattled and a book fell from the bookcase. Before Kimsey could speak, the newcomer advanced until his face was close to Kimsey's. "Kimsey, for Chrissakes, it's my life you bastards are playing with! I've been fucked around pretty good in my time, and by experts. But nothing compared to the way we were shoved onto that beach. Which Goddamn genius said we were going to be the torch that would set Cuba alight! I want one hell of a lot of answers, Kimsey, and, by God, if they're the wrong ones, I'll have someone's balls. You'd better read me, Kimsey. And read me well!"

His voice was low-keyed and murderous, the accent elusive. Even in rage, he was in complete command of himself. His hands on Kimsey's desk were clenched, the knuckles white.

He had glanced once, piercingly, at McDonald, and then ignored him completely.

Abruptly the man turned his back and stormed out of the room as violently as he had entered.

McDonald said, "Jesus, Herman, I feel as if I'd been hit by a truck."

Kimsey shrugged his shoulders. All he said was "Yeah."

"Is he one of yours . . .?"

"He's an assassin," Kimsey said shortly, "maybe one of the best there is. He works for a lot of people."

McDonald knew he wasn't going to get any more, but Kimsey said, "He's got a beef . . . and I think maybe he's right."

"Well," McDonald said, "I'm glad it's not *my* balls he's after."

Kimsey shook himself, rose to his feet, gathered

20

several papers from his desk, others from a drawer, and slid them into a neat brief case. He adjusted his tie inside his button-down Brooks Brothers collar, and put on his jacket. He was instantly transformed into an executive.

"Sorry, Hugh, the debriefing calls, and it will be a rocky one. How long will you be in town?"

"I don't leave until June."

"Good. Give me a call. Let's get together and talk about the good old days."

Kimsey's clichés, after the scene he had witnessed, scraped like tin on glass. McDonald left the building deeply disturbed.

The Washington spring day was balmy, giving promise of great heat in the months to come. The CIA had not yet moved to Langley, Virginia, and McDonald hailed a taxi giving the driver the address of his apartment. He sat back and reached for his cigarettes. And then he felt an extraordinary and totally unexpected sensation. Reaction. As he lit his cigarette he saw that his hand was shaking.

He realized he had had an experience he would not forget.

Within a few days he was once more caught up in his principal line of work. McDonald was, is, and always will be—a cop.

At that time he was a chief in the Los Angeles County Sheriff's Department. His studies at the FBI National Academy were interrupted by a wire from Sheriff Pitches, his Chief in Los Angeles. McDonald's reputation was such that his assistance was frequently requested by Police Departments all over the country.

This time it was a small Southern town. They had a case that baffled them completely—the violent murder of a state Beauty Queen.

21

III

April, 1961

It was the kind of case a detective hates. It was six weeks old. All the investigation that could be done on it while it was hot, or even warm, was done. Furthermore, Hugh McDonald was a big-city boy, used to the tension and hostilities of Los Angeles and Chicago. He was not used to the closely-knit atmosphere of a small town, where the Sheriff was known to everyone by his first name, and the older people had known the local policemen since they were kids.

The town had a population of about eighteen thousand. McDonald's first talk with the Sheriff took place on the steps of the courthouse in the morning as people were going to work. Their conference was constantly interrupted by hails and greetings like "Take it easy, Frank," and "Have a nice day now, Mabel." There was no cop-hating here.

But the Sheriff knew his job. The Police Department had done its homework. Still, after six weeks they were baffled. And that was why Hugh McDonald was called in.

The victim was a former beauty queen, twenty-seven years old, married to an administrator who worked on an Army post. They had no children. They lived in a modern, two-bedroom bungalow with an attached garage in a new community some distance from town. The victim worked in a doctor's office, but had been home for several days recovering from the flu.

Suspicion had immediately fallen on the husband for the uncharacteristic way he had behaved on the day of the murder. He had come home for lunch because, he told the police, he was concerned about her. But then, according to his testimony, he did not return until ten o'clock that night. He said there was a movie he wanted to see at the Army theater. He did not telephone his wife. He parked the car in the garage, let himself into the house by the kitchen door, stepped in, and found his wife stabbed to death. Her housecoat, her only garment, had been almost ripped off. Her head was bludgeoned in, but she had not been sexually assaulted. Nothing had been stolen.

The couple were generally considered to be happily married, and there was no record of infidelity on either side.

There was blood all over the house. The victim had fled from the attacker. But there was no evidence of house-breaking. The victim had *not* been surprised by the presence of her attacker. She had been killed between three and four o'clock in the afternoon.

From these premises, McDonald set to work reconstructing the scene. It was broad daylight. The attacker comes to the front door. Although the beauty queen is naked except for a housecoat, she does not hesitate to let him in. Shortly afterwards, for some reason, a struggle begins. She flees. The murder instrument is one of her own kitchen knives, so the killer arrived unarmed. After she fell, dead or dying, he grabbed a hammer used for breaking ice, and bashed her head in.

The girl had been buried a month, so McDonald ordered a mock-up, and draped the housecoat over it. She was tall, five feet six inches. He gauged the angle of the knife-thrusts. Had the attacker been a short man, the knife would most likely penetrate the body straight in. A tall man would bring the knife down at an angle, particularly if both were running. McDonald and the Sheriff then agreed that the assailant had to be at least six feet tall. The girl's husband was short, which cleared him.

McDonald was delighted with the Sheriff's cooperation. It was a tenet of his faith that it takes two to solve a difficult crime. In the words of one of McDonald's lectures, "One must follow a pattern of logic acceptable to others besides oneself. Another brain is needed. I found this out at both the FBI and the CIA. Don't work for yourself. Be sure another mind is in agreement."

The next point was to assemble a physical picture of the man. He would probably be of medium build because both McDonald and the Sheriff conceived of him as young, agile enough to chase his victim round the house and still keep enough wind to stab and bludgeon her.

It was McDonald who mused, "Young . . . young . . . Sheriff, it was a *kid*." He reasoned as follows: an older, stronger man would have struck her down in the living room, preventing her from fighting back or fleeing.

The girl saw the boy approaching the house, had no fears about admitting him. As the boy was unarmed, he planned no violence. Something happened that led to unpremeditated murder.

This narrowed the investigation with a vengeance. The high schools of the town were checked for any boy absent from class at the time of the murder. Within weeks he was caught, a boy fourteen years old, six feet tall, a star athlete from a nearby town. As they say in the Deep South, poor white.

His confession corroborated McDonald's analysis. The boy wanted money, and had knocked on the first door he saw. The girl, probably thinking he was the paper boy, admitted him. His demand infuriated her. She slapped him. The boy panicked, thinking she might telephone the police for attempted robbery. He had never been in trouble before. He knocked her down. She rose and fought back, screaming, "Get out of here, you young punk!" She broke free and ran to the kitchen, to get a knife. He reached it first. After she died, he spent an hour cleaning up the house, wiping up blood, replacing furniture. Then he left, and made his way home, stealing nothing.

It was characteristic of Hugh McDonald, when asked what happened to the boy, to say, "How would I know?" His mind was so disciplined by his métier that, once his part of the job was done, he put it out of his mind, and went on to the next problem.

IV
Los Angeles
November 22, 1963

Promotion came swiftly for Hugh McDonald. In 1961 he was named Division Chief in the Los Angeles County Sheriff's Department. He recalls that he was sitting in his office at the Sheriff's Department when the first garbled accounts of the attempt on President Kennedy's life came through.

In those early reports, the newscasters knew only that John Kennedy had been shot in Dallas' Dealey Plaza. The extent of his injuries was not known—nor whether he would live or die.

McDonald remembers that he sat glued to his desk radio as further reports came in; the President was badly wounded, but would live; the President had suffered brain damage, extent unknown—and finally that John F. Kennedy, the thirty-fifth president of the United States, the leader of fabled Camelot, was dead.

Like so many of us, Hugh McDonald wept.

He wept again as he watched the TV coverage of the funeral cortege, the prancing black stallion with empty saddle and boots turned backwards, the street lined with silent mourners.

But, unlike most of us, he was filled with a cold professional rage as TV showed him the inexcusable murder of Lee Harvey Oswald—a man was,

26

from McDonald's lifetime of training, "presumed to be innocent, until proven guilty."

It was with immense satisfaction that he read a week later of the appointment of the Warren Commission. Chief Justice Earl Warren was something of an idol of his.*

True, McDonald was somewhat puzzled at the attitude of the new President, Lyndon Baines Johnson, who first proposed that the Commission be composed entirely of Texans to inquire into an assassination which had taken place ". . . deep in the heart of conservative . . . Texas . . . ."**

Then Chief Justice Warren clearly showed his reluctance to head the Commission.***

McDonald wondered why.

---

*McDonald says, "Only a quirk of history prevented Warren's reaching the White House. He ran with Tom Dewey against Harry Truman in 1948, when Dewey was defeated in the upset of the century. Had Dewey won, he would have run again in 1952, and probably won. Precedent would then have given Earl Warren the chance to run in 1956, and he would probably have won, too. Eisenhower would have remained a soldier, and Adlai Stevenson would have remained Governor of Illinois."

** William Manchester, "The Death of a President," 1967

****The New York Times* quoted Warren when President Johnson sent Solicitor General Archibald Cox and Deputy Attorney General Nicholas Katzenbach to ask if he would head an investigation of the facts of the Kennedy assassination. "Tell the President," Warren said, "for personal reasons, I do not wish to serve on such a commission. Tell him also that the Court does not look with favor upon extracurricular commissions of that kind. I myself am averse to it. It was only when the President requested that I visit him at his office and he told me of the wild stories that were going around the world and of what this might mean internally if there was not a thorough probe of the facts, and some conclusion reached as to who was responsible for the assassination, that I agreed to serve. He thought that no less a personage than the Chief Justice of the United States should head it up. I remember him saying, 'You served the country in uniform, and this will be a more important service than anything you could do in a uniform.' So I said, 'Mr. President, in spite of my strong reluctance about the matter, if you consider it of that importance, I will do it.'

Professionally, McDonald was familiar with the investigative agencies, the CIA and the FBI. He considered them, and still considers them, the best in the world, better than Scotland Yard, or the French *Duexieme Bureau* or *Police Judiciaire*. He had worked with them all, and respected them deeply. The American investigators would certainly bring to the Warren Commission all the facts. McDonald also trusted, albeit with some reservation, that the Commission would draw the correct conclusions.

V
July, 1964
Washington, D.C.

In July, 1964, the Sheriff of Los Angeles, Peter Pitches, called McDonald into his office, and told him the Republican National Committee wanted him to assume direction of security control for Senator Barry Goldwater and his running mate, Congressman William Miller, for the duration of the 1964 Presidential campaign.

This was an honor indeed. It would make McDonald the second most important bodyguard in the United States, second only to the officer directing the security of the incumbent, President Lyndon Baines Johnson. Yet, for reasons not connected with the story, McDonald was not immediately enthusiastic. His mother had just died at the age of 93, and he was deeply grieved. But, on the urging of his elder brother, he agreed.

Here is a crossroads as spine-tingling as any in history. Had he declined the job, this story would never have come out.

At the expense of the Republican National Committee, McDonald flew to Washington, where he was interviewed by Denison Kuetchil, John Grenei, and the National Chairman, Dean Birch. The interview was short, friendly, and positive. McDonald requested, and got, a starting budget of $75,000. He needed some immediate money, in cash, which was also supplied. He appointed as his deputy an old colleague, Mel Lind, and the two of them headed back to California to assemble a team. They were scheduled to pick up Senator Goldwater at the Illinois State Fair in three days' time.

In the 727, McDonald and Lind talked strategy. No matter how many toes had to be stomped on, no harm must come to the candidates. McDonald said, "Mel, we can't guard Goldwater against every crank, nut or martyr in the world. Someone might kill him. But, by Christ, Mel, you and I won't be alive to see it, because they will kill us first."

"You're the boss," said Lind, sounding less than delighted at his putative immolation.

Forces, disparate and in considerable numbers, were coming together now to direct Hugh McDonald to his quest for, and tracking down of, President Kennedy's killer. The basis of his assignment was the vogue for political assassination in general. It had become an important factor in political life.

McDonald and Lind set up an office on twenty-four hour duty in Washington, D.C. And who should be the first to enter his security network but his old friend, Herman Kimsey! He had left the Company and was working for a private investigation agency run by Leonard Davidov, considered one of the top electronics experts in the world. McDonald took them both on his payroll.

He ultimately built a team of ten crackerjack detectives, one from Florida, several from the Middle West, a couple of Easterners and the rest from the Los Angeles area, all personally and professionally known to McDonald.

McDonald recalls Senator Goldwater's surprise when he presented his team of bodyguards. The

Senator had not realized that such elaborate protection was necessary, and he did not like the idea. It was not McDonald, but Charles Justice, Goldwater's special aide de camp, who persuaded him. The Senator insisted that he would accept no restriction on his freedom of movement. McDonald said nothing but intended otherwise.

Every Sunday morning the McDonald team was briefed on the week's schedule, and the day was set aside for tactical and strategic planning which sent the men fanning out across the country as advance parties and watchdogs. McDonald had two men with the Senator all the time, even when he was resting. McDonald was usually in the plane with him, though keeping himself free to rush to any emergency.

McDonald says, "It is hard for the average American to believe this, but there was not a single city or town the Senator visited in which he did *not* receive threats on his life. Don't forget, in that campaign, he generated a great deal of hostility from many directions: from anti-Viet Nam war groups; from the Left generally; from people still grieving for John F. Kennedy. Goldwater was running not only against Lyndon Baines Johnson. He was running against Camelot and the ghost of Kennedy. He was not a favorite son in the East, where the howling down of Nelson Rockefeller at the Republican Convention was considered a scandal. Goldwater was blamed for everything. Many of the threats came from cranks. But it is, alas, cranks who kill."

Cranks . . . and professionals, with high-powered rifles, telescopic sights, and the promise of much money.

Akron, Ohio, was a case in point. Several threats had come from Akron. Instead of riding with Goldwater in his plane, McDonald took the press jet because it arrived first. His advance man, Hank Matheny, retired lieutenant, Santa Monica Police, had been advising him daily that the threats were piling up. Matheny and McDonald examined all the physical security precautions, checked with local police, studied the barriers to hold back the crowd, checked sight-lines from the upper windows of buildings.

Nor was assassination the only menace. Akron was Middle America, where Barry Goldwater had a big following. Enthusiastic crowds could press on him, crush him and perhaps injure him seriously.

The tactics on arrival were as follows: One of McDonald's men, usually Prell, would be first to appear at the open plane door. He would scour the waiting crowd looking for McDonald or one of the other men. If the "all clear" signal was flashed, the Senator's arrival would take place as planned. There were several signals. If McDonald signalled "unsafe," the Senator would be held aboard the plane until the "all clear" signal was given.

One of the rules was that the security men never went in front of the Senator. That was on Goldwater's orders. They never imposed themselves between the Senator and the camera, or the people he was greeting. They flanked him from behind, four or five paces away, always at least two, sometimes three. They never looked at the Senator, only at the crowds, their eyes alert for any suspicious movement. Should anything happen, one man was always poised to hurl himself in front of the Senator.

As Goldwater proceeded from the plane to the automobile, the tactics changed. One man or two men were always in the campaign car. The others rode in a car beside him. Some watched windows only, others only the crowd.

At the halls in which he spoke, the problems were different again. Here the angles *inside* the location were the places offering a sight-line for a rifle. McDonald said, "At first I couldn't analyze my own feelings when we finally got back aboard the plane and buckled our seatbelts, until I recognized them. I felt as I did in World War II, like a soldier waiting for a fire fight. It was a kind of weakness at the knees."

And then, in McDonald's own bailiwick of Los Angeles, they nabbed one.

A night rally was arranged for Dodger Stadium. Up to forty thousand people were expected to attend. Herman Kimsey was sent on ahead for a dry run along the Goldwater motorcade route, studying points where security would be particularly vulnerable. Afterwards he confessed to McDonald he was particularly worried about an area on the side of the hill, overlooking the stadium, near the gate by which Goldwater would enter. And Kimsey was right. Not only was a car parked and a man seated inside: he carried a rifle. But three of McDonald's men were there too, and made a Citizen's Arrest.

VII
Dallas, Texas
September, 1964

The Los Angeles incident proved to be too much for Herman Kimsey. They were on their way to . . . Dallas. As part of his dry-run supervision, he took McDonald to Dealey Plaza, told McDonald what he knew, pointed out the building from which President Kennedy was shot, not the famous window in the Book Depository Building, or the floor from which Lee Harvey Oswald fled. The shot was fired from the second floor of the Records Building, across the street from the Book Depository.

The two returned immediately by taxi to their hotel. McDonald telephoned room service for ice, poured himself a drink, then settled himself for a long session. He forgot to order coffee for Kimsey, so Kimsey ordered some for himself. It seemed almost as though they wanted to prolong the moment of truth.

McDonald will never forget his intense excitement: the manhunter's indescribable elation when he feels he is close to the end of the trail, the answers to the puzzle about to unfold.

"All right, Herman. Let's have it all."

Kimsey stood looking out of the window, and McDonald realized for the first time that this was a habit of his when under stress.

"The reason I am telling you this, the reason I took you to Dealey Plaza, was because you—and I—have the responsibility for Senator Goldwater's safety. The odds are on President Johnson, the polls are for Johnson—but we have had upsets before. And—if there is even a bare chance that the Senator might win this election, there's a possibility the same mechanic might be employed again to do a job on Goldwater."

McDonald considered. "Herman, how did you get your information?"

"He told me himself, from beginning to end. How he was hired to assassinate the President, how Lee Harvey Oswald was set up as the patsy. Everything."

"It makes no sense, Herman. *Why* did he tell you?"

"I think he had to . . ." Kimsey said slowly. "Look at it *his* way . . . The prime target. The biggest hit in history. The President of the United States . . . the *United States!* Jesus! He had to tell *somebody!*"

"You must have known him very well," McDonald said.

Kimsey looked away. "I knew him. Yes, you could say that. I knew him."

Kimsey sat down in an armchair and closed his eyes. He spoke. He spoke for three hours. Kimsey's voice was reduced to a hoarse whisper. When it was over, the story was complete in every detail, all the questions were answered, and for the first time everything about the President's assassination made sense.

The two men sat for a long time in silence. At last McDonald said, "What are you going to do with it, Herman?"

"I don't intend to do anything with it, Hugh, and furthermore, I don't intend to let *you* do anything with it. If you tell this story to a living soul, I shall deny it, and you will come out looking like a horse's ass. I'm working for you now, and I *owe* it to you. You have to protect Goldwater's life, and should have every bit of information available. But that's all."

"Listen, Herman . . ."

"No more questions. I've said everything I have to say."

McDonald said, "No, you haven't. Do you think the Company was involved in the murder?"

Kimsey sat up, rigid, furious. "Are you crazy? Of course not! This man was a free lance, open to offers. Someone hired him. That's not the way the Company operates. That's one of the reasons that this story has to be kept quiet. No matter how it came out, the image of the Company would be seriously hurt."

McDonald knew his friend well, knew his intense loyalty to the Central Intelligence Agency, but he still wasn't prepared to let him off the hook. "Next question, do you think any other part of our government was involved in the killing? Or was it an outside job?"

Kimsey took longer to answer than he should have, and McDonald was immediately suspicious about what he would say.

"I'm not sure I have the answer to that question. When he first talked to me about it, he felt there *might* have been a government connection. You know the rules of the game, Hugh. On a job like that, the less one knows, the better.

"He finally came to feel that the man who hired him was working for a private group, but that group had strong government connections."

"You mean, *our* government?"

"Damnit, Hugh, don't jump to conclusions. He first met the man who hired him to kill the President in 1961, at the staging camp in Guatemala for the Bay of Pigs invasion. At that time, at least, he felt this man had a connection with the U.S. Government. When he saw him next, it was in Haiti, and the meeting took place in a house that could have been United States Government property of some kind."

"And the man never said who he was representing?"

"Why the hell would he want to know? If he knew, the information would be his death warrant. I told you—the man *said* that he was *not* representing *any* government, and the assassin came to believe that a private group was behind it."

"Jesus, Herman—you *must* realize you can't just leave it there!"

But Kimsey did.

He said only one more thing before he left.

"If anything should happen to me . . . go to Len Davidove. He will have my notes, and my files . . . I'll see to it."

Dusk was falling. In the quiet of early evening, the traffic noise from below seemed almost oppressive. McDonald needed time to digest the fantastic story he had heard.

He was too tired to piece the thing together. The business at hand took precedence over the story he had just heard. He had enough of a job getting Senator Goldwater into and out of Dallas vertical and in one piece, while exposing him sufficiently to satisfy his supporters.

VIII
Fall, 1964
Presidential Security

The job of protecting Barry Goldwater now took on a vastly deeper dimension. McDonald fought down a sensation that was not far removed from panic. Oswald was a crank; Oswald did not kill Kennedy. A professional assassin killed Kennedy; if there were private business interests rich enough to pay, a professional killer could kill Goldwater. All the "theories" of the Kennedy assassination faded into fiction. McDonald did not, for one moment, believe that a paid assassin, having pulled off the coup of the century, would risk his luck a second time. He had identified himself too clearly by his style, and that style was known to at least one former senior officer of the CIA. But there were, as Kimsey said so chillingly, other mechanics, perhaps not better, but as good.

Suddenly Goldwater seemed terrifyingly exposed. McDonald's team, so carefully selected, seemed puny to protect him from a cold, deadshot rifleman whose bullet might come out of nowhere.

In the light of what he had learned, McDonald now began to worry about something he had previously shrugged off as human nature, namely the hostility of the law-enforcement officers in some towns and cities. In these strong Democratic districts, when they called on the local police for reinforcements, they would be told that none could be spared; all were busy. Frequently they were told, "Don't tell *us* what to do. This is *our* town." Everywhere they went they were strangers, and unwelcome strangers. They were even strangers to the man whose life they were paid to protect. Goldwater, like all top politicians, had definite ideas on how things should be done, and blew up—not often, but enough to increase the tensions of the job.

McDonald had set up a color identification which was not always welcomed by local plain-clothes men. This consisted of a lapel button of a certain, variable color. "Look at it this way," he said to the grumblers. "If there is a shoot-up, I don't want to shoot you, and I would like to think you would prefer not to shoot me. These buttons mark the team."

But the job had to be done, and the work went on. New York, with its usual sophistication, understood McDonald's problems. The Commissioner assigned the entire New York Command Staff to him, and said, "Tell them what you want." McDonald recalls New York as the only place the Senator visited in the entire campaign where he, McDonald, felt reasonably relaxed.

On a train carrying the campaign party from Los Angeles to San Diego, McDonald received a warning from the Secret Service that military supplies, including hand grenades, had been stolen from a local Marine base. McDonald had to figure that one out from scratch. How, in God's name, did one protect Senator Goldwater from a grenade flying through the air while he was making a whistlestop speech? A man with a gun is, by definition, visible, providing one is looking in the right direction. A grenade can come lobbing out of a crowd.

41

McDonald's solution had a somewhat kamikaze air about it. One of his men would have to go. One would be standing behind the Senator on the rear platform as he made his speech. A second man would alight on the tracks, beside him. The first man would field the grenade as it flew through the air, or pick it up if it fell. In one single sweep he would toss it to the man on the track who would throw it *under* the train. The mass of metal wouldx be protection enough against the blast. As McDonald told them, "The Senator must not die. One of us may have to."

McDonald recalls their worst scare, in Cleveland, Ohio. A man had written a letter announcing his intention to kill Goldwater. The Secret Service warned McDonald that the man was dangerous, and had been imprisoned once for threatening the life of Lyndon Johnson. McDonald was personally on patrol outside Goldwater's hotel suite when one of his men rushed up and said, "He's here. He just checked in."

With reinforcements of local police they smashed into the suspect's hotel room. He was gone. An *empty* rifle case lay on the bed. Goldwater was due to speak in thirty minutes, in an open-air amusement park. McDonald says, "This time I was prepared to stop the Senator, even if it meant the use of force. I had to tell him, 'Senator, we are going to surround you whether you like it or not. Furthermore, we will all be carrying rifles.' "

Goldwater, a political giant with a keen sense of realism, understood the danger, and reluctantly agreed. McDonald did not tell him his next stratagem, because he knew the Senator would never accept putting someone else's life in danger.

The speech went off without incident. Goldwater

left for the car which he would share with political dignitaries. Instead, and to his astonishment, he was hustled by McDonald into another, more modest car. The arclights and floodlights were dimmed, and Bert Amio, wearing clothes like Goldwater's, and thick horn-rimmed-looking spectacles, took his place in the campaign Cadillac. McDonald recalls with some satisfaction, "I thought he would hit the ceiling. But he just sat there, looking into space, trying to understand. The Senator had a fine war record, and was a brave man. I think this was the first time he really understood the serious danger he was in. We rushed him to the airplane, and he mounted the steps and entered it without a word to the local politicos seeing him off. The only time, so far as I remember throughout the campaign, that he didn't give a farewell to them."

And incidentally, the suspect was never caught, and may still be planning political murder today.

McDonald says, "I think it was this incident, this threat of death, which changed our relationship. He had said some pretty rough things to me—I won't quote them—and I resented them. He said I was screwing up his campaign-style, inhibiting him, and getting in his hair. I muttered some pretty nasty things about him under my breath nights as I flung myself on my bed and tried to sleep an hour or two. Then I began to admire him, and he seemed to begin to respect me. There was never any real fellowship or rapport between us, just the realization of shared pressure. I voted for him in the election."

Every Friday night, a private jet collected the entire team, no matter where they were, and flew them back to Washington for a briefing which lasted until the small hours of the morning in clouds of impenetrable cigarette smoke. Saturday they rested, and Sunday they were on the road and in the air again. McDonald estimates they logged ninety thousand miles, or a thousand miles a day.

McDonald and some of his men were still with the Senator on Election Day, at his home in Arizona, and they and a handful of supporters sat around on the patio. Goldwater was listless, drained, and knew he was beaten; all those speeches, all those flights, and train journeys, television appearances, all that handshaking, and all those confident smiles, all those entrances into and exits from the Valley of the Shadow of Death. And in the end, he had lost.

McDonald shook hands with him. "Thanks, Hugh," Goldwater said. "You did a great job. I'm alive, aren't I! And thank all your boys. Have a good rest now."

For the record, Hugh McDonald wants to acknowledge the work of his team; professionals in investigation, interrogation and law enforcement—amateurs in security matters, but not for long: Melvin Lind, Leonard Davidov, Hank Matheny, Bert Amio (retired Captain, Los Angeles County Sheriff's Department), Jack Prell (Chief of Police, Florida State University), Bob Gogamas, Herman Kimsey, and Harry Crager.

IX
The Warren Report
Exhibits and Evidence

Kimsey's shocking revelations during the Goldwater campaign served to make McDonald even more anxious to read the final findings of the Commission.

When the Warren Report was finally released, McDonald spent many hours analyzing it. Above all, he wanted to believe it—and not Kimsey's fantastic tale. But his policeman's mind had a lot of questions.

By all accounts, Oswald was a poor shot. Some time before the assassination he had missed an easy standing target when he took a shot at Major General Edwin Walker* in Dallas. How could any one explain the deadly accuracy and unbelievable speed of the Dallas killer?

Like many other experts, McDonald was particularly disturbed about the ballistics testimony, its contradictions and, in some areas, its downright absurdity.

Both the Secret Service and the FBI reported to the Commission that three shots had been fired from the back, two hitting the President and one hitting Governor Connally.

*April 1963

Then McDonald came upon the findings of Arlen Specter, one of the Commission's lawyer-investigators. Specter was presenting the theory that the first bullet hit the President, passed through his upper back and came out at his lower throat area. Then, that same bullet plunged into the back of Governor Connally, broke a rib, exited and then hit his right wrist. What came to be called "the miracle bullet" wasn't finished yet, according to Specter. It went on into Connally's right thigh (where it left a piece of itself imbedded in a thigh bone) and ended up on a stretcher on which Connally was carried into the hospital.

McDonald didn't have to be a ballistics expert to realize that this must have been the strangest bullet in history because the picture of the bullet showed that it was nearly totally in it's original shape. It was so clean that it must have been fired into a ballistic box of cotton, water, or some other soft material.

Then McDonald spotted something he had missed before: photographic exhibit number 237. He got the shock of his life. The face in the photograph was unmistakably the man in Kimsey's office; the man Kimsey claimed had actually shot Kennedy.

What in Hell was this unidentified man doing in the middle of the Warren Report—unless Kimsey's story was true!

Frantically, he went through the surrounding exhibits, hoping to find something . . . anything . . . which would tell him more.

What he found was something else entirely. A statement by Richard Helms, Deputy Director of the CIA, that:

1. The picture was taken October 4, 1963, in Mexico City.

2. He had never seen or heard of the man in the picture, and had no idea who he was.*

3. Two FBI agents, Bardwell Odum and James Malley, didn't know who it was, either.

AFFIDAVIT OF BARDWELL D. ODUM

The following affidavit was executed by Bardwell D. Odum on July 10, 1964.

PRESIDENT'S COMMISSION
OF THE ASSASSINATION OF
PRESIDENT JOHN F. KENNEDY

AFFIDAVIT

STATE OF TEXAS.
County of Dallas, ss:

I, Bardwell D. Odum, having first been duly sworn, depose as follows:

I am presently a Special Agent of the Federal Bureau of Investigation, U.S. Department of Justice, and have been employed in such a capacity since June 15, 1942.

On November 23, 1963, while acting officially in my capacity as a Special Agent of the Federal Bureau of Investigation, I obtained a photograph of an unknown individual, furnished to the Federal Bureau of Investigation by the Central Intelligence Agency, and proceeded to the Executive Inn, a motel at Dallas, Texas, where Marina Oswald was staying.

In view of the source of this picture, and, in order to remove all background data which might possibly have disclosed the location where the picture was taken, I trimmed off the background. The straight cuts made were more quickly done than a complete trimming of the silhouette and I considered them as effective for the desired purpose.

I desired to show this photograph to Marina Oswald in an attempt to identify the individual portrayed in the photograph and to determine if he was an associate of Lee Harvey Oswald.

It was raining and almost dark. I went to the door of Marina Oswald's room and knocked, identifying myself. Marguerite Oswald opened the door slightly and, upon being informed that I wished to speak to Marina Oswald, told me that Marina Oswald was completely exhausted and could not be interviewed. Marguerite Oswald did not admit me to the motel room. I told her I desired to show a photograph to Marina Oswald, and Marguerite Oswald again said that Marina was completely exhausted and could not be interviewed due to that fact. I then showed Marguerite Oswald the photograph in question. She looked at it briefly and stated that she had never seen this individual. I then departed the Executive Inn. The conversation with Marguerite Oswald and the exhibition of the photograph took place while I was standing outside the door to the room and Marguerite Oswald was standing inside with the door slightly ajar.

Attached hereto are two photographic copies of the front and back of a photograph.* I have examined these copies and they are exact copies of the photograph of the unknown individual which I showed to Mrs. Marguerite Oswald on November 23, 1963.

Signed this 10th day of July 1964.

(S) Bardwell D. Odum,
Bardwell D. Odum

AFFIDAVIT OF JAMES R. MALLEY

The following affidavit was executed by James R. Malley on July 14, 1964.

PRESIDENT'S COMMISSION
ON THE ASSASSINATION OF
PRESIDENT JOHN F. KENNEDY

AFFIDAVIT

DISTRICT OF COLUMBIA, *ss:*

I, James R. Malley, Inspector, Federal Bureau of Investigation, Department of Justice, being first duly sworn, depose as follows:

In accordance with a request by Mr. Howard P. Willens, a member of the staff of the President's Commission on the Assassination of President Kennedy, I transmitted to the Commission on February 11, 1964, a copy of a photograph of an unidentified man which was made available to the Federal Bureau of Investigation by the Central Intelligence Agency.

Prior to transmitting the aforementioned copy of this photograph to the President's Commission, I used a scissors and trimmed from the photograph all background which surrounded the head, shoulders and arms of the unidentified individual. I did this, inasmuch as the Central Intelligence Agency had previously advised that it had no objection to this Bureau furnishing a copy of this photograph to the President's Commission with all background eliminated.

I have examined a copy of Commission Exhibit 237, which is attached,* and it appears such ex-

---

*The photograph referred to in the above affidavit of Inspector James R. Malley is identical to Commission Exhibit No. 237 and appears in the exhibit volumes.

hibit was made from the copy of the photograph of the unidentified individual which I cropped and transmitted to Mr. Willens on February 11, 1964.

To my knowledge, the identity of the unknown individual depicted in the copy of the photograph which I transmitted to Mr. Willens on February 11, 1964, has not been established.

I have reviewed the records of the Federal Bureau of Investigation in this particular matter and such records disclose that a duplicate copy of this same photograph was cropped in a different shape to remove background by Special Agent Bardwell D. Odum of the Dallas Office of the Federal Bureau of Investigation and was then exhibited to Mrs. Marguerite Oswald by Special Agent Odum on November 23, 1963.

Signed this 14th day of July 1964, at Washington, D.C.

(S) James R. Malley,
James R. Malley

AFFIDAVIT OF RICHARD HELMS

The following affidavit was executed by Richard Helms on August 7, 1964.

PRESIDENT'S COMMISSION
ON THE ASSASSINATION OF
PRESIDENT JOHN F. KENNEDY

AFFIDAVIT

State of Virginia,
County of Fairfax, ss:

Richard Helms, being duly sworn says:

1. I am the Deputy Director for Plans of the Central Intelligence Agency.

2. I base this affidavit on my personal knowledge of the affairs of the Central Intelligence Agency and on detailed inquiries of those officers and employees within my supervision who would have knowledge about any photographs furnished by that Agency to the Federal Bureau of Investigation.

3. I have personally examined the photograph which has been marked Commission Exhibit No. 237, a copy of which is attached to the affidavit of Inspector James R. Malley, dated July 14 1964, and the photograph attached to the affidavit of Special Agent Bardwell D. Odum dated July 10, 1964.

4. Those photographs are partial copies of a photograph furnished by the Central Intelligence Agency to the Federal Bureau of Investigation on November 22, 1963. They are referred to as partial only because, on information and belief, Odum and Malley personally trimmed or cropped their copies of the photograph to exclude the background against which the individual portrayed in these photographs is depicted in the original photograph.

5. The figure portrayed in those photographs is the same individual portrayed in the original photograph.

6. The original photograph was taken outside of the continental United States sometime during the period of July 1, 1963 to November 23, 1963.

Signed, this 7th day of August 1964.

(S) Richard Helms,
RICHARD HELMS

Saul, as shown in Warren Commission Exhibit #237. Saul identifies this picture as being taken at the Russian Embassy in Mexico City, either in the foyer or just outside.

Hugh McDonald gave copies of this photograph to Blue Fox contacts during his search for Saul.

McDonald knew he had to find out more about the man in the picture. He began to tap the sources of information he had built up over the years. Most of his conversations began with, "I hate to remind you—but you owe me one. And this is important . . ."

This is the story of the mystery picture, the sum of what McDonald found out, much of it at the time, some of it much later.

On October 4, 1963, somewhere in Mexico City, a covert photograph was made by CIA agents. For some reason, the agents involved in making the picture thought that they were photographing Lee Harvey Oswald.

On the morning of November 22, 1963, *before the assassination,* a copy of that picture was received by the FBI in Dallas, Texas. The picture was identified as *possibly* being Lee Harvey Oswald. The FBI agents in Dallas knew Lee Harvey Oswald, and they knew that the photograph forwarded to them was *not* a picture of Oswald. At the time this error in identity did not seem important. However, things changed radically after the killing of President Kennedy and the apprehension of Oswald for that crime.

Months later, the Chief Counsel of the Warren Commission, J. Lee Rankin, wrote to the Deputy Director of the CIA, Richard Helms, requesting that all of the information on the photograph be given to the Warren Commission. It finally was, and with a number of crucial deletions, the documents were supplied to the Commission. They did *not* supply an uncropped copy of the picture.

In secret FBI reports, it appeared that three pictures of the mystery man were shown to a Mexican national, Mr. Pedro Gutierrez Valencia. They were

Saul, in one of the photographs recovered from the Federal Bureau of Investigation. Obviously, this photo was taken with a covert camera and has also been cropped.

shown to him hoping that he could identify the man in the picture. He could not. This is, however, the first information that reveals the existence of other and different pictures of the same unidentified man. So far as can be ascertained, the other pictures of this man were never shown to the Warren Commission. Mr. Valencia described *three* photographs as follows:

Number 1: A man attired in a white shirt and tan trousers, holding what appears to be a courier-type pouch under his left arm and examining a wallet-type folder which it appears may contain one or two documents resembling passports.

Number 2: The same man attired in the same dress described above and holding the wallet-type folder in his left hand and inserting this folder into the courier type pouch held in his right hand.

Number 3: The same man attired in a dark shirt with white collar buttons and apparently walking along with the thumb of his left hand hooked into the top of his left hand trouser pocket.

The unidentified man in the photograph became important as a possible co-conspirator of Oswald. The FBI felt that it was necessary to identify the man in the picture. Agent Bardwell Odum showed the picture to Marguerite Oswald, Lee Harvey Oswald's mother. She said that she had never seen the man in the photograph. Odum tried to show the photograph to Oswald's wife, Marina, but she was exhausted by all of the events and could not be disturbed or interviewed.

On the 24th of November, Jack Ruby shot and killed Lee Harvey Oswald. Mrs. Marguerite Oswald then identified the picture shown to her by Agent Odum as *Jack Ruby*. This was the second erroneous identification of the mystery man. The CIA had named him Lee Harvey Oswald and

Saul, in the second photograph taken by the Federal Bureau of Investigation. The Warren Commission was not aware of the existence of these two pictures.

Oswald's mother had named him Jack Ruby. The man in the picture was still a mystery.

Exactly when and where was the picture taken? On July 22, 1964, Richard Helms, then the Deputy Director of the CIA and later the Director of that Agency, signed an affidavit that the photograph was taken on October 4, 1963, in Mexico City.

The photograph in its entirety was never shown to the Warren Commission on a voluntary basis. On February 11, 1964, upon the request of the Commission, the FBI sent a copy of the picture to the Commission. This copy had been trimmed down further—eliminating *more* background—at the request of the CIA.

It would appear then that there are at least two agencies who were interested in identifying the man in the photograph, and that interest extended far beyond the time when Oswald was considered to be the only assassin.

Who was the man in the picture?

It was at this point that McDonald gave his mystery man a name. He called him Saul.

To this day he can't remember why, unless it was the Bible: "And Saul caused Uriah, the Hittite, to be placed in the forefront of the battle . . ."

McDonald's faith in his sometime employers, the CIA, was shaken to the core. An outright lie couldn't be covered by the tattered blanket of "national interest . . ."*

---

*"I still believe," McDonald says now, "American investigation is the best. But my admiration is no longer blind. Every day, the press and television reveal how sacrosanct agencies have been tampered with, especially in the Kennedy, Johnson and Nixon years. When that happens, the temptation for the preservation and obstruction of justice is very real. Worse, honorable and distinguished men, sensing miscarriage of justice, find it more judicious to turn their heads away. Rather than intervene, they prefer to know nothing. It happens every day in the Soviet Union. It happened in Hitler's Germany, and in Mrs. Indira Gandhi's India."

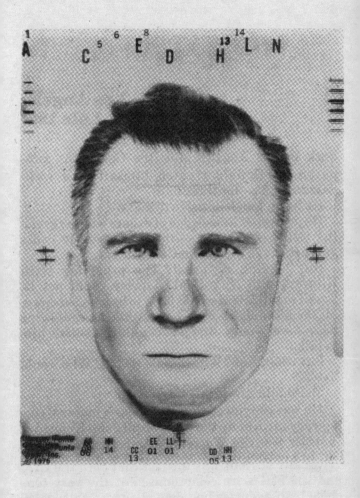

Identi-Kit Model II composite of Saul compiled by Hugh
McDonald from memory of the 1972 meeting at the Westbury
Hotel in London.

X
Los Angeles
Late 1964

Back in Los Angeles after the Goldwater campaign, McDonald treated himself to a well-deserved rest—for three days.

He had a tough decision to make.

He possessed knowledge of events whose revelation could shake the world—and possibly cause grave damage to his own Government.

But he had no proof. The proof lay with Kimsey—and with Saul. Kimsey could not be forced to talk. Saul would have to be tracked down. McDonald had no real doubts that he could find Saul—eventually. And just possibly persuade him to talk.

But what then? Whom could he tell? Who would listen?

McDonald saw it this way:

He was convinced that there was a massive conspiracy to cover up the truth about John Kennedy's murder. Was the Warren Commission, knowingly or unknowingly, patently a part of it?

Equally obvious was the fact that both the CIA and the FBI were compromised at the very top, since both agencies had denied any knowledge of Saul. At this point McDonald was not prepared to believe there had been actual complicity from either agency. But, even so, there was no denying that *nobody* wanted to hear any more about Saul. So that avenue was closed.

What was really behind the assassination?

There were several possibilities.

Other governments: The Vietnamese. If they believed that Kennedy was responsible for the overthrow and murder of President Diem, they might have acted in revenge. But if that were the case, surely they would want the world to know about it.

Cuba's Castro: Perhaps in retaliation for the Bay of Pigs, and the various attempts on his own life, which he attributed to the U.S.

Disaffected Cuban refugees who blamed Kennedy for pulling out of the Bay of Pigs invasion.

But in any of these cases—why the cover up? It didn't make sense.

After he was forced to rule out the CIA, the FBI and the Warren Commission, McDonald had seriously considered going directly to the President with his information. It could be done. McDonald had enough clout to get an interview.

What stopped him was a very sobering possibility—which *did* make sense. According to Herman Kimsey, it was Saul's strong impression that the assassination had been arranged by a private group. If that were so—then there was one glaringly obvious reason. These men, whoever they were, preferred Lyndon Baines Johnson as President of the United States to John F. Kennedy. Taking it one step further, McDonald wondered that if these people removed Kennedy because they couldn't do business with him, did they believe they could do business with Johnson? If that were true . . . then approaching the President could be very dangerous indeed—if not fatal.

At this stage of the game, McDonald refused

even to speculate about who the omnipotent "they" might be.

McDonald has the tools of his trade in abundance—an infallible memory, a burning curiosity, and tenacity which would put a bulldog to shame. But in this case he was up against forces he couldn't buck. With great reluctance he decided to give it up and get back to work.

It was work with a capital W. At that time McDonald was Chief of Detectives of the Los Angeles County Sheriff's Office, commanding six hundred men. He had a full lecture schedule on various phases of Police Science at the University of Southern California, Long Beach State College, Pasadena City College, The University of Oklahoma—and Scotland Yard. He spent his spare time turning out such standard texts as *Classification of Police Photographs, Investigation of Sex Crimes,* and *Practical Psychology in Police Interrogation.*

He still managed to get in some time in the air as Commander of L.A.'s Aero Squadron.*

For relaxation he worked on polishing and perfecting the Identi-Kit.**

---

*McDonald is still an active flight instructor on fixed-wing planes and helicopters. He holds multi-engine rating and instruments rating. He, along with Earl Brown, former TWA Captain, developed a special police plane, the Sky Sentinel, whose most outstanding feature is its silent flight. Its communications and optical systems are so sophisticated that they can pick up house and license numbers from the air.

**This device has been called "the greatest thing for police identification since fingerprints." It took McDonald twenty years to develop it. It all fits into a little black box—536 four-by-five-inch photographic transparencies. McDonald's work began when he was a twenty nine-year-old detective in the Identification Bureau in Los Angeles. He felt that if the endless variations of human fingerprints could be precisely coded and transmitted all over the world—then why not faces and

"Twelve years later," McDonald says, "I knew it would work. But that's all I had—faith. I was fresh out of money and manpower, and my fellow cops were beginning to call me a nut. I was about to call it quits and throw the whole thing in the ashcan, when the Noville people came along. Rex Noville was Admiral Byrd's pilot over the South Pole. He was found dead, shot through the head, shortly before the assassination," McDonald adds.

Noville provided him with all the equipment and funds he ever dreamed of. Five years later he had fifty thousand transparencies of faces sorted, dissected and indexed. The slides showed 130 different hairlines, thirty-seven noses, 102 types of eyes, fifty-two chin shapes, forty sets of lips—in addition to all sorts of beards, mustaches, eyebrows, scars and headgear.

The system worked beyond all expectations.

Identi-Kit is now standard equipment for Police forces all over the world, including Interpol. It has been responsible for the identification and apprehension of thousands of criminals.

On the evening of January 17, 1967, more than three hundred people attended a party in the Pacific Room of the Statler Hilton Hotel, at Figueroa and Wilshire Boulevard, Los Angeles, California. The occasion was the retirement —premature—of Hugh C. McDonald, Chief of Detectives, County Sheriff's Department, the fifth largest law enforcement agency in the country.

That evening he received the following telegram:

---

heads. He began by dissecting hundreds of head shots into their component parts, nose, eyes, lips, chin, eyebrows and hairline. He became convinced that the system was manageable, that there *were* precisely describable elements in every adult human face.

Hugh C. McDonald, Chief of Division
Sheriff's Department, Los Angeles Co.,
Calif.

Dear Chief,

On your retirement I want to express my appreciation for all the assistance you have furnished my associates in the past. We have long valued your wholehearted cooperation and will certainly miss the fine relationship we have enjoyed with you. All of your friends in the FBI join in extending best wishes for continued success, and we hope your future will be filled with much happiness.

Sincerely yours,
John Edgar Hoover
Director, FBI

McDonald says, "I'd been splitting myself twenty ways for far too long. I felt it was time to get out of active duty. My outside interests were demanding all of my time—and I wanted to see something of my family." (McDonald has six children.)

Immediately after retirement, McDonald went to work for the Howard Hughes Tool Company, flying and demonstrating their Model 300 Sky Sentinel helicopter to law enforcement agencies across the country. He stayed with them six months, then moved to the Chicago area, where he became Director of Security for the Midwest Bank Card System.

While in Chicago, he received a telephone call from Leonard Davidov, the electronics expert for whom Herman Kimsey worked after leaving the CIA. Davidov wanted McDonald to come to

Washington to be interviewed by *U.S. News and World Report* about security measures in the upcoming election. McDonald declared, and was so quoted, that security should be in the hands of experts, not amateurs; otherwise, no candidate was safe. He was particularly emphatic about what he called "the antics" of Bobby Kennedy on the campaign trail. Citing his Goldwater experiences, McDonald said, "We seem to be a nation with more than our fair share of kooks. Assassination is in the air. Any candidate who refuses to take sensible precautions for his own safety is a damned fool—and is courting a bullet." He was thinking about Saul, at large, prowling, a dead shot and open for offers.

McDonald was in Chicago on June 5, 1968, when Robert Kennedy was shot in the Hotel Ambassador. At two in the morning the telephone rang. *U.S. News and World Report* told him of the assassination and asked his views in the context of his earlier prediction. McDonald recalls, "My instant reaction was not the grief I felt when Jack Kennedy was killed. It was one of rage. I told the reporter that Bobby Kennedy got exactly what he was asking for. For months the man had been disregarding even the basic demands of prudent security. His approach to the problem was reckless, so Goddamn reckless, it was enough to make many a thinking man in grave doubt about his credentials for the Presidency. Once again, our Presidency has been stolen from us."

Back in Los Angeles, McDonald had made himself into something of an expert on the art of political assassination.

He says: "The killer whose motive is simply money is the one who causes all homicide men to

65

lose a lot of sleep. This expert 'mechanic' gets his down payment, and begins to study his target. He works by his own timetable, picks the place and the circumstances, makes his hit, collects the rest of his money, and—zip, he's skiing in St. Moritz before the corpse is cold. We can take all sorts of sophisticated precautions against the nut—the deranged martyr who is *looking* to be caught. And most of the time we can stop him. But there's damn little we can do about the 'mechanic.'

"The White House Detail concentrates heavily on the guy with the high-powered rifle with telescopic sights. And so they should. But there are a lot of other ways to eliminate a target that aren't so spectacular.

"The Russian hit squads have used the cyanide gas weapon for years. It's easily concealed, silent and totally effective. You don't even have to *breathe* cyanide. It can penetrate any mucous membrane, eyes, lips, nostrils—or a cut in the skin—and kill in seconds. The Russians even invented a solution which neutralizes skin contact for the 'mechanic.'

"Now, even the cyanide gun is old hat. The latest wrinkle is an air-propelled needle capsule, which can go through clothing (up to almost thirty yards) and enter the body with no more pain than an insect bite. It's like a cold capsule. It can take up to twelve hours to release its poison. By that time the 'mechanic' is once more in Timbuktu.

"So clean. So quiet. All traces of poison disappear within sixty minutes. And the autopsy report invariably will say 'heart attack.'

"There is still official suspicion about Adlai Stevenson, who dropped dead on a London street. It could have happened the way I've described."

Some years ago, McDonald was involved in the investigation into the supposed suicide of James Forrestal, Secretary of the Navy under President Roosevelt and Secretary of Defense under Harry Truman. On May 22, 1949, while the Secretary of Defense was undergoing a routine check-up at Bethesda Naval Hospital, he suddenly jumped out of a window to his death. Official verdict: Suicide.

McDonald was approached by a Federal agency and asked to join an investigation. The agency questioned the suicide verdict. It was their belief (and many still believe it) that Forrestal was the victim of a carefully covered professional assassination. Their behaviorism profile of the Secretary of Defense indicated that he was not the kind of man who would take his own life under any circumstances.

"Nowadays," McDonald says, "everyone knows what visual subliminal suggestion is—pictures flashed on a screen so fast that the eye cannot record them, but the brain, which has a much faster reaction time, can. The viewer doesn't know what he's seen, but the message is firmly embedded in his mind.

"At the time, few people were familiar with the technique. The Russians were. I happened to be familiar with a series of experiments the Soviets had made. *They* approached subliminal transmittal through the *ear*, rather than the eye. Like the principle of the 'silent' dog whistle.

"On the audio spectrograph there is a range where you're not conscious of hearing—yet your brain *does* hear. If I know your range, I can flash a message to you electronically and make you act on it.

"It's my understanding that it was tried out at a

football game. The guinea pig had no idea that they were flashing a message to him to get up and leave the stadium. It was a pretty exciting game, yet the man got up and left—under audial subliminal suggestion. He had completely lost the power to control his own actions—and he never even knew why he had left his seat.

"That's what I think happened to Secretary of Defense James Forrestal. He was subliminally controlled—and *compelled* to leap to his death."

It was only after Robert Kennedy's killing that Hugh McDonald became completely convinced that, sooner or later, he would have to find Saul —and prove or disprove Herman Kimsey's story. He couldn't live with himself if he didn't.

In the meantime, he waited for the next assignment which would take him to Europe.

XI
September, 1970
London, England

It wasn't until 1970 that the cards fell right for McDonald to start his search. Early in September he received a cryptic phone call. The caller was a woman, and she used an identification phrase that was all too familiar to McDonald—although he hadn't heard it in years: Jug-head.

What the woman said was: "If you will be at the Polo Bar at the Westbury Hotel, on Conduit Street, Mayfair, London, at 8:00 on the evening of September 26, you will receive information which is vital to your Government."

McDonald briefly checked his calendar and said, "Not unless I know a little more about why I'm coming."

The distant voice said, "It concerns the island of Vozrozdenya, in the Aral Sea. We believe the Russians have a germ warfare installation there."

"Spell it," McDonald said. And then, "I'll be there."

He then placed a routine call to his contact at the Central Intelligence Agency and told him what had occurred. He got the go-ahead—which wasn't really necessary, because McDonald had decided to go anyway.

The recognition phrase the anonymous woman

had given McDonald took him all the way back to Hitler's Germany, just after the fall in 1945. At the time, McDonald was an officer in the 314th Military Government Detachment. His assignment was to find whether Adolf Hitler had really died and been cremated in that famous bunker at the Reich-Chancellor Building.

His next job took him to Augsburg to establish a law enforcement safety division. This police group is the present Landpolizei Schwaben.

During these two assignments, McDonald came into contact with a number of interesting people, people who had one thing in common—a fear and hatred of Soviet Russia. They were Poles, Czechs, Rumanians, Germans, Scandinavians and two Russians. Twelve in all.

These people were dedicated to the proposition that the Soviets must not be allowed into Europe—and then into the rest of the world—a proposition with which McDonald was totally in sympathy.

These people, men and women, enlisted more than McDonald's sympathy. They asked and received his active help and advice in forming an organization for the sole purpose of observing, analyzing and reporting all future activities within Russia and the Russian sphere of control.

"In 25 years," McDonald says, "the group has grown. Some of them have died, some retired—and some have given their lives for what they believed in. The survivors have bred sort of a second generation. Some of them were active in the Berlin revolt, and later in Hungary and Czechoslovakia.

"I believe these people can penetrate the Iron Curtain better than any other group in existence today.

"I have renewed contact with them on occasion, when my work has taken me to Europe. They still know me as one of the 'Founders.' It is through them that I have sources of information from deep inside Russia."

McDonald calls this network of dedicated agents by the code name of "Blue Fox."

"These people are not funded from the U.S., nor do they have any connection with any U.S. agency. Nor, to the best of my knowledge, are they connected in any way to any foreign government. I do not know where they get their major financing. I have never inquired. Their information has been made available, from time to time, to many of the intelligence agencies of the major western countries.

"I do know that most of them have legitimate jobs, and support themselves. They all, without exception, abhor and fear the Communist ethic."

McDonald makes no bones about one overwhelming political prejudice. He loathes and detests detente and all it stands for; progressively emasculating and debilitating the United States while the Soviet Union sucks at American strength, growing stronger and stronger abroad and increasingly tyrannical and oppressive at home. He considers Kissinger wrong, Nixon a crook and Ford inadequate.

On September 24, 1970, when Hugh McDonald left for London, he was carrying Saul's picture in his briefcase. He planned to show it to certain people. This, in itself, was breaking all the rules.

A basic tenet of intelligence work is that an agent works on only *one* job at a time. Usually it is only one *segment* of a job, and he does not go one inch beyond that segment. An assignment must be clear-cut, well-defined and have a fixed termination point. An agent does exactly what he has been told to do—no more, and no less. For all he knows, there may be twenty other agents working on the overall job. A deviation by any of them could blow the whole works—months, even years, of effort.

Whatever it was that Blue Fox had to tell McDonald must be important—for their request for a meeting was unprecedented. Any mention of something extraneous to their present mission could well silence Blue Fox entirely.

Knowing this, McDonald decided it was a chance he had to take.

If Blue Fox agreed to help him, McDonald had a fair idea of what reaction to expect once the word of his hunt for Saul spread out.

McDonald says, "I did not even know Saul's name. But then, he did not know mine. He was a contract man for the CIA. But then, so was I. He did dangerous jobs for private interests. But then, so did I. We swam in the same pool, and it was only a question of who got to whom first."

McDonald felt he had one unique advantage. He had lived with Saul so long that he believed he could literally read Saul's mind. It was similar in so many respects to his own.

When Saul learned that he was being tracked, he would say, "Someone is on your heels, kill him." And then, "No. Two can play this game. I want to know why—and what he knows. If this man is stalking me, I can stalk him. If, after I know what he wants with me, it becomes necessary to kill him, I shall kill him. But, in the meantime—I am . . . curious." McDonald had to pray that he was right.

Before he left for London, McDonald checked the Encyclopedia Brittanica, and then the Los

Angeles City Library, libraries at the University of California, the University of Southern California, the Library of Congress, the files of the National Geographic Society, and the New York Public Library. When he got to London he tried the Royal Geographical Society and the Reading Room of the British Museum.

No Vozrozdenya.

What the maps did show were tiny unnamed islands in a rough circle off the northeastern shore of the Aral Sea. One of them had been named, by someone, Vozrozdenya.

On September 26th, McDonald waited impatiently in the Polo Bar of the Westbury Hotel. His contact was fifteen minutes late. At 8:20, a well-dressed young man approached his table and sat down. McDonald had never seen him before—but the recognition phrase the man murmured, Jughead, was all too familiar.

The young man examined him in silence. McDonald was puzzled by the man's expression, until, with some surprise, he realized that it was curiosity tinged with admiration.

"Forgive me," the young man said. "You are something of a legend to many of us. I had never thought to meet you."

McDonald remembers a mild embarrassment, and the thought, "Jesus, am I *that* old?"

What the young man told him didn't surprise him, but it did have a certain shock value. He learned that on the island of Vozrozdenya in the Aral Sea, germ warfare was being planned against the United States.

McDonald says that if any reader of this book has suffered, in the last five or six years, from what he thought was London flu, or Hong Kong flu, and found his friends and colleagues sniffling in the same way, it is quite possible that they were in fact the guinea pigs of Vozrozdenya.

What McDonald learned back in 1970 is still true today.

The Russians transmit the germs in the jet stream, which passes from east (Russia) to west (the United States). The operation is diabolically simple. Small missiles are introduced into the jet stream, carried by it to the U.S. Once there, these missiles are timed to release their nasty cargo over any given section of our country. The shock value in what the young man told him was that the Soviets had now gone far beyond the simple nuisance of a flu bug. They were experimenting with lethal germs.

What the Russians were doing could not be disguised or euphemized as providing benefits by discovering antidotes for disease. The experiments were sheer deviltry, designed to incapacitate—and perhaps eventually to kill—large segments of the American population, just in case the need for such an operation ever arose.

He learned that Vozrozdenya is a very small island, and the most carefully sealed and guarded piece of real estate in the world. The Aral Sea lies about three hundred miles east of the Caspian Sea, east of the Ust'-Urt Plateau to the north. The sea is about a hundred and seventy miles wide, and rather more than two hundred and fifty miles long. "On the island," the young man said, "they do their testing on human guinea pigs. Recently we were able to remove one from the island.

"We picked him up, and we got him out of Russia. Unfortunately they know we have him. At present he is in hiding somewhere between the Russian border and West Germany.

"We think we can get him out—and you can hear his story personally . . . if we are lucky. The search for him is intense. That's all I can tell you at this time. Now, you must go to the Continental Hotel in Zurich. You will be contacted there."

McDonald debated briefly whether to show Saul's picture to this man, and then decided to take the chance.

The young man studied the photograph. "This is a dangerous man. What is your interest in him?"

McDonald lied. "I know he is dangerous. That's why I want to contact him. I have a job, work for him to do. How do I find him?"

The contact shook his head. "No. I'm not even sure I know him. My remark that he is dangerous is based on two things. Analysis of the photograph. He *looks* a dangerous man. And the fact that the photograph is in your possession compounds it."

McDonald did not believe him, acknowledging to himself that neither did the contact believe McDonald. But before they shook hands, the man asked to keep the picture. "Sure," said McDonald. "I have plenty more. Will you find him for me?"

The reply rocked McDonald to the core. "Does your interest in this man have anything to do with the murder of your President in 1963?"

McDonald gulped, but hoped he succeeded in sounding casual. "No. I told you. I want to talk business with him. Why on earth did you ask that question of all questions? Do you know something I don't?"

The young man rose. "You are treading on dangerous ground, my friend. Leave it alone. Go to Switzerland."

He left through the swing door. McDonald was absolutely certain that the man knew Saul. Whether he would pass on the word, McDonald had no way of knowing. But McDonald was now sure that Saul was reasonably well-known in highly specialized circles on the continent of Europe. The ball was rolling.

Normally, the investigative process seeks patterns of behavior in crime. A detective soon reads the "handwriting," as it were, of a professional safecracker or bank robber, or, for that matter, a hired killer. He leaves the same mark, the diploma of his talent. Saul was an ace shot. McDonald knew the kind of gun he preferred, the kind of preparations he made, his pattern of exodus after the crime is committed.

But a man shoots a President once in a lifetime. Saul was unlikely to shoot another. His next victim might be a trade union leader in Buenos Aires, a nosey politician in Sicily, a business man in Australia. The net was too wide for McDonald to check him out by dead reckoning. He could only hope—and wait for the breaks.

In the meantime, there was Vozrozdenya.

XII
October, 1970
Zurich, Switzerland

In Zurich, McDonald checked into the Continental—and waited. He could do nothing until he was contacted. It was two days before they showed. This time it was a woman, an attractive woman in her early forties. The two sat in her car, parked near the Zurich Sea opposite the Eden au Lac Hotel. The time was shortly after four o'clock in the afternoon. Rain fell in showery patterns. The sky was covered in heavy, dark clouds, with patches of blue sky peeping between them. The temperature was in the sixties and a blustery wind shook the stationary car.

McDonald's description of the lady is purposely vague. She is still active with the Blue Fox organization. She was friendly and animated.

She told him that the organization had managed to move their guinea pig much closer to the West German border. At the same time the hunt for him had intensified. The Russians were most anxious to get their hands on him. Time was on their side, for the man was very ill. If he could not be moved across the border in the next few days he might die.

McDonald was to go to Augsburg, in Bavaria—and hope for the best.

"Don't worry. We will get him out."

Somehow, McDonald believed her. He felt cheered by the interview.

Until he showed her Saul's photograph.

Her face became a mask. She looked at McDonald, and said in a voice of steel, "I was sent to give you certain information. No one told me there would be a query about this man . . ." she waved at Saul's picture, ". . . or anyone else, for that matter."

McDonald felt guilty. The lady had a right to be angry. He had broken the rules, and his conscience was far from clear.

"It is important I contact the man in the picture. I believe he is known in Europe. You and the organization are the only people I can turn to. I don't want to get anyone into trouble, but I have no alternative."

She was not impressed. "Maybe we can, and maybe we can't. Right now, you and I are both involved in an operation that has already cost us some lives. Frankly, I don't give a damn about your interest in this man. Finish the job you are doing first. Later we might be able to help. Who knows?"

She drove McDonald back to the hotel. They did not talk on the way. Oddly enough, it was this woman, so hostile and businesslike, who would later play an important role in the final identification of Saul.

XIII
Augsburg
West Germany

Augsburg. McDonald's old stamping ground in World War II. He went first to the office of the Land Polizei, at number 2 Konigsplatz.

The headquarters were still in the same place as they were in 1945. Augsburg had been more or less untouched by the bombing. The Chief of Police greeted him as an old friend. Within hours he was surrounded by middle-aged and elderly men and women who had worked with him in 1945 when he was forming both the Land Polizei and the watchdog counter-espionage of Blue Fox against the Russians.

He passed a pleasant few hours, and then went to check into the Weisse Lamb Hotel, a small, decent place in the heart of the city, to await his contact.

It came earlier than he expected, at ten thirty in the morning. The telephone rang in his room and a man spoke. Without preamble, he said, "Meet me in the lobby of the Drie Moren Hotel in one hour. What is the exact time by your watch?"

"Twenty eight minutes to eleven." McDonald was used to the question. Time is always the first part of a "Phase" contact to ascertain positive recognition.

The voice said, "Walk through the main entrance at exactly eleven by your watch. Proceed to the center of the lobby. Drop something, anything, on the floor, stoop over, pick it up, and then walk back to the main entrance."

"And your signal?"

"I will hand you a bright yellow pencil. Then follow me back into the hotel. We will talk in my room."

The orders were obeyed, and it wasn't until 11:45, after waiting to ascertain an "all-clear," that McDonald and the contact were seated with Scotch and soda in a room on the third floor of the hotel. The contact was a small, stocky man, with well-cut clothes.

"In two days we will have him out. Or he will be dead. You are to go to Garmisch-Partenkirchen to the Mark Platz Hotel. Someone will reach you there and take you to him—if he's still alive.

"You must forgive us for the seeming chase you have followed. Believe me, it was necessary."

McDonald said, "It's not unusual. I have been through similar operations before."

"But you cannot know how closely we are watched—even here in West Berlin. In the meantime I have information for you."

The small man laid a map on McDonald's lap. It was hand drawn, but with a cartographer's skill. It listed each building in the scientific complex on Vozrozdenya—and its function; the laboratories, the two crematoria for the human guinea pigs who succumbed, the protective radar screens —and described the most elaborate and complete security system McDonald had ever seen.

"The scientists live in a tiny community called Rybachy Posela. There is a missile station on the mainland about thirty miles southeast of Vozroz-denya. The missile station is small, and does not carry intercontinental missiles. From time to time, it has been noted that scientists, carrying small packages, take the daily steamer from the island to the missile station.

"The missiles are fired vertically into the air, not on any angled trajectory. They are not capable of reaching any great distance.

"But—a big but—the launching site is directly underneath the main jet stream. Furthermore, the co-relation between activity on Vozrozdenya and new types of influenza in America is disturbingly exact.

"We believe that soon you may be getting something considerably stronger than influenza germs. Such is the price of friendship with Mother Russia."

McDonald thanked him and assured him that he would be in Garmisch, only a few hours away by train, at the appointed time.

Before McDonald could produce his picture of Saul, the man beat him to the punch. "I hear you are hunting for a particular man in connection with some other activity."

"Correct. Can you help?"

"What is his name?"

"I haven't the slightest idea."

"I am not enthusiastic about this, you know. Our contact in Switzerland said you have a photograph. I am curious."

McDonald produced Saul's photograph. The small man studied it for a long time, and handed it back. "He is dead. You will not find him. He came from Russia. I met him first in 1949, right

81

here in Augsburg. He was a displaced person. I heard maybe two years ago that he had been killed in Mexico."

McDonald was stunned. The hunt was over. The last and ultimate witness had joined the ranks of the Kennedy dead. McDonald had no doubt that the man believed what he was saying. Nevertheless, he pressed. "This is very important to me. Are you sure?"

"No."

"So why . . . ?"

"I can't even remember where I got the information. But that is the situation as I know it. In our business, as you know—we hear these things. Now you must leave." He stood up, walked over to the door, and held it open.

XIV
Garmisch
West Germany

McDonald spent that evening with his friends of the Land Polizei getting very drunk indeed. He remembers singing the old songs, and at one point in the evening quietly weeping, as though he had lost a friend.

As a consequence he didn't arrive in Garmisch until the evening of the following day, after a jolting train ride which was no help to his aching head.

Somewhere, during the short trip, his hopes revived.

After all, there was no *proof* that Saul was dead.

He registered at the Mark Platz, and checked into a large, old-fashioned room on the second floor. A French window led out onto a small balcony with a stupendous view of the Zug Spitz, the highest mountain in Germany, more than ten thousand feet high.

He remembered Garmisch from World War II days. It had never been bombed, and tourism had not really spoiled it. The people, costumes, atmosphere, remained unchanged.

That night an attempt was made on his life.

At about ten o'clock at night, he went to the bar for a nightcap, Kirsch and a beer chaser. He returned to his room up a broad, creaking staircase.

The rooms are comfortable but the doors do not close tightly at the Mark Platz. He opened the double windows onto the balcony and stood for a few minutes enjoying the sparkling mountain night air. He left the windows open, took off his clothes and crawled into the wide bed, under the eiderdown which Germans prefer to blankets.

McDonald never sleeps in a dark room. It is his habit to arrange for a slim light between him and any door leading to his sleeping quarters. Even in an airplane, he leaves his reading light on. This is known professionally as the Shadow Alarm. Anyone entering passes between the object of attack and the light. The professional is thus instantly awakened.

The room in the Mark Platz did not permit a Shadow Alarm. Instead, McDonald left the light on in the bathroom. He then spent ten minutes in the darkness, another habit, checking and classifying all sounds outside his room, the opening and closing of doors, the traffic in the street below. These were filed into his brain on some kind of list of "expected sounds." They would not wake him. But the brain remained alert for "unexpected sounds."

For some reason, McDonald was nervous when he went to bed. He was unarmed. Except in rare circumstances, he never took a gun with him when he went abroad. Should he be arrested by the authorities in some covert activity, he could always hope to talk his way out of trouble, providing he was unarmed. A gun was his confession of guilt, and perhaps his death warrant.

After filing every sound outside his room in his mind, he now checked the position of each object in the room. In his state of tension, everything seemed to have taken on a new clarity in which objects are seen like a flash of lightning; his brown suit hanging on the dumb valet, tailored for him by Hayward of Mount Street in Mayfair; his brush and comb set on the chest of drawers, given to him at some Christmas or other; the polished brown shoes extended by shoe trees; his briefcase on the floor, decorated with an old red, white and blue sticker of the S.S. France. Should any object be moved even fractionally while he slept, he would know it immediately on wakening.

He put on pale blue pajamas, bought at a Tripler's sale in New York, and went to sleep.

And suddenly he was wide awake. Something had triggered his alarm system, and he did not yet know what it was. He was lying with his back to the door, and the faint light from the bathroom gleamed on a mildly sensual print of nymphs and satyrs hanging on the wall. The sensation that had waked him was a slight draft between the open door and the open window to the balcony. Someone was standing close to the bed, behind him, leaning over. His heart pounded. He was agonizingly aware that, by awakening, even though he had not moved, the somnolent rhythm of his breathing had been broken. He sensed movement and then felt the cold, razor-sharp edge of a knife against the side of his neck. The voice was a whisper. "You have come to the end of the road, mister."

It all happened so rapidly, McDonald did not know if the words had penetrated his sleep or if he was awake when he heard them. To the end of his days he would never be able to assert whether they were uttered in English, Russian or German.

He moved with the speed of terror. He rolled, not away from his assailant, but toward him. The direction of the move took the man by surprise, and skin contact with the knife was mercifully lost. McDonald brought his pajama-clad knees to his chest, and kicked out hard. The heels caught his assailant in the pit of the stomach, and smashed him against the wall near the door. McDonald was on his feet, dizzily, smashing hard and blindly with both fists. One landed beautifully on the man's face, a punch to remember and savor. It sent the man staggering out of the room. McDonald slammed the door, and leaned against it until his breathing and heartbeat eased. He could hear the man running down the creaking corridor and galloping down the single flight of stairs to the lobby.

McDonald ran over to the balcony. A few seconds later he saw a man leave the hotel, a handerkerchief to his nose as if to stanch blood. He walked with jerky motions, like a man forcing himself not to run. He turned a corner and disappeared in the direction of the gambling casino.

On shaky legs McDonald walked to the bathroom. His watch showed 2:45. A bottle of Schnapps stood on a shelf along with his toiletries. With a hand that trembled, he poured a heavy slug into a glass and drained it, coughing at the impact of the powerful liquor. The mirror showed him a thin line of blood running from under his ear around to his Adam's apple. If he had rolled in the opposite direction, away from his assailant, his throat would have been slit.

McDonald sat in an old leather armchair. His cigarette glowed in the darkness. He sought to put the pieces together. This was not by any means the first attempt on his life, although one always hoped it would be the last. Of one thing he was absolutely certain. That, dead or alive, Saul had nothing to do with it. The knife was not Saul's weapon, nor was the bungled lunge. If Saul were alive and decided to eliminate him, McDonald would never know it. A rifle with telescopic sights, a bullet through the brain. And Saul would be out of the country in an hour.

XV
Garmisch
The Contact

The next day was one of the longest McDonald could remember. The attempt of the night before convinced him that Soviet agents were determined that he never meet with the Vozrozdenya patient. If they couldn't find the man themselves—then they would make sure that McDonald wouldn't either.

He felt completely exposed and helpless. They knew where he was, and he couldn't make a move. He had to stay in his hotel room until someone made a contact with him.

The telephone rang sharply, and McDonald almost jumped out of his skin. It was 4:20 P.M.

A man's voice said, "Sie sprechen Deutsch?"

"Naturlich."

"My name is Ernst. What is yours?"

"Hugh."

"Hoog?" The voice was puzzled. The name was a tongue-twister in any European language.

McDonald spelled it.

"H-u-g-h."

"What is your second name?"

"That is none of your business."

There was a pause, and the voice was aggrieved. "I don't have to see you, Hoog. You answer the questions, and leave the remarks to me."

He was right. The man was cautious because his life could be at stake. McDonald was immediately contrite. "I'm sorry," he said. "I've had a tough day. They took a run at me last night. Tell me what you want me to do, and I'll do it."

"I know," the man said. "Now listen. Leave the hotel, and walk north. Watch your right hand side. Look into the store windows. When you come to the first jewelry store ... " McDonald was always enchanted with the German word for jewelry, *schmuck,* " ... you will see a large clock in the window. It is not running. The hands are set at exactly two o'clock. Sitting beside that timepiece, there is a smaller clock, running. Stand in front of the window looking at the big clock at exactly 5:00 p.m. by the hands of the small clock. At that time, I will appear in the window, and move the hands of the big clock to the time of four o'clock. Study me so that you will recognize me. Do you understand me, Hoog?"

"Yes."

"Walk to the Bahnhoff, and buy a ticket for the cog train, the funicular, which takes you to the summit of the Zug Spitz. At 5:20 I will be at the ticket window buying a ticket to the same place. From that point on, do not lose sight of me. Do not approach me, just keep me in sight. When I go into the restaurant at the hotel, follow me and sit at the same table. If, by any chance, I do not appear at the ticket window of the funicular, return to the hotel and wait for another contact. Do you understand me?"

"Clearly."

Ernst hung up instantly. McDonald now had a fairly good idea why the man was being so excessively cautious. They had heard from other

89

sources about the attack on his life, and were trying to protect him.

The instructions slotted in at every point without a hitch, and by 5:45 McDonald sat opposite his man by a vast picture window with a brilliant, dizzying view of the towering snowcapped peaks.

McDonald was surprised at the age of the man. His telephone voice suggested a man in his thirties. Ernst was well over sixty, but carrying the pink, pure complexion that comes from a lifetime of breathing mountain air. His body was firm and without excess fat. His voice was soft but authoritative. "You must not be impatient with us. You are in danger. You are watched. We must all be cautious. The information we have for you has taken many months to acquire. Yesterday a very important courier for us was devoured by guard dogs on the Hungarian border. The East Germans think up new tricks all the time. They have turned the Curtain into a real curtain, a curtain of shimmering steel slivers. It looks rather pretty. The slivers are sharper than razors. Just to touch will sever a finger. They placed the order with a West German firm, and paid for the merchandise in West German marks. Isn't life strange?"

McDonald heard him, and felt ashamed. And helpless. These people were front-liners, combat troops in the lonely world of covert intelligence gathering. There were no hurrahs, just work, disappointment, frequently death. While he, McDonald, was putting them to extra danger for what they could legitimately consider was a private vendetta between Hugh McDonald and this man called Saul.

"We got him out—but only just. He hasn't long to live. In a few minutes I will take you to him. He will tell you what he knows in front of witnesses—and we will record what he says to you. We will give you our own depositions so that there will be no question of authenticity. We will make certain that you leave this country safely. After that it will be up to you."

XVI
Vozrozdenya
The Statement

It happened just as Ernst said it would. By round-about ways, McDonald was taken to a house on the outskirts of Garmisch. There, he met a man who was obviously dying. Another unsung hero.

Part of the man's statement follows. His explanation of how he left the island has been changed for obvious reasons.

"In the summer of 1970, I became very ill with radiation sickness after working in the mines. My sickness caused such concern to the doctors that I was taken away from the work roster and put into the hospital. On the third or fourth day I was removed from the hospital on a stretcher and flown in a small aircraft with Soviet Air Force markings to an airport near what I later learned was the Aral Sea. I was transferred, still on a stretcher, to an even smaller aircraft where I was the only passenger, and flown to the island of Vozrozdenya. I was given to believe by the women doctors who treated me that this was a hospital which specialized in cases of radiation sickness and that I would be well looked after by famous doctors.

"On the landing strip at Vozrozdenya, I was taken from the stretcher and helped into a small automobile, and driven to a medical center in the little town.

"I was interviewed at great length by three Russian specialists, two of them men, one a woman. It was the first time I had any experience with male doctors in the Soviet Union. They are nearly all women, and usually very gentle. The name of the three doctors were Emile Kroptate, Peter Gorsach and Marion Lentzen. They were pretty stern with me at first. They told me I was not a civilian patient. I was a German prisoner of war who, as a soldier, had invaded Russia—which was not true, because I had been captured in Berlin, and had never set foot in Russia except as a prisoner of war. They shipped us all out to Siberia.

"They then said I had some claims to redemption because I had worked in their mines. As I had acquired a Russian girl friend in the process, I had not asked for repatriation when the time came up, and this also was considered a factor in my favorable treatment.

"They then got to the point, and it seemed to me they had some difficulty in speaking up. They told me they needed human bodies for experiments. Only that way could they get to the heart of treatment for radiation sickness. Dr. Marion Lentzen took my hand. She said, 'We want to use your body. If you don't allow it, you will die, because we can't cure you. If you allow us to experiment on you, we may be able to develop a cure. You will be released, and not only given your passage to Germany, but also take your girl friend with you. This, as you may or may not know, is not a privilege often accorded by Soviet authorities. If you agree, and if we succeed, you will also be awarded a medal. If we do not succeed, I am afraid you will die, but you will die knowing that your death has added to human knowledge, and that others who fall ill with the same illness as you may be cured.'

"I was feeling as low as I could be. I set no store on my life. Dr. Lentzen was quite pretty, so I thought, what the hell, let her go ahead and experiment on me. It was all the same to me.

"I had to sign scores of forms, and though by now I could speak Russian, I still couldn't read it very well, so I had no idea what I was signing. That night, I was given a comfortable bed and a sedative. Next day I was given a check-up that lasted several hours. I was returned to my room, given books in German, published in East Germany, novels and so on, and East German newspapers to while away the time. I was also given a long smock and slippers to wear.

"Next day—the same thing. More tests, X-rays, pain killing pills, some fairly conventional treatment to keep my temperature down. I was feeling pretty rotten.

"The thing went on and on, every day for more than a month, and I must say at the end, thanks to treatment, I was feeling quite a bit better.

"And then quite suddenly everything changed. I felt worse, drastically worse. I had been given pills, injections. I had swallowed various fluids, and digested something that tasted like a chocolate malted milk. I developed a cracking headache, and they would not give me aspirin, or anything to end it. I should also tell you I was kept as a prisoner. My room was always locked, although I had a call bell which was always answered by a medical orderly as soon as I pressed it, and everybody was very courteous. The food was reasonable, a bit starchy, but from the time I got there I had very little appetite. God knows how much weight I lost.

"I rang the bell to complain about this headache of mine. The orderly—his name was Ivan; by now we were on first-name terms—read from a chart which I could see was not the same as it had been before, a different color and size. He said that no prescription had been written in. I had to put up with the headache, and it would go away in time.

"I spent a dreadful night, and I knew my temperature was rising. By morning I was on fire. Ivan brought me in my breakfast, the usual thing, a glass of tea, plenty of bread, and a little fish. I couldn't eat. I couldn't move. I think Ivan was really scared by my condition. He took the breakfast tray away, and in a few minutes I seemed to be surrounded by doctors. I may be wrong. They may have been the same three, but there were also others, young, maybe interns, or students. I was too weak and feverish to know or see.

"They checked me and they seemed particularly excited by the rise in my blood pressure. After an hour's examination, maybe more, maybe less, but a long one, they gave me a hypodermic which knocked me cold. I slept all day and all night, and by the following morning I felt I could climb a mountain.

"Dr. Lentzen came in with a vase of flowers, and asked me how I felt. I said I felt great. Then she asked me something strange. She asked if I smelled anything in the room. She did not mean the flowers. I said I didn't. She asked, did I have any difficulty in breathing. No, I was breathing normally.

"She then took a clipboard and asked a lot of

questions. When did the headache start? I told her. She asked me to describe it, writing everything down. I told her it all began with a slight pain in the back of my head. I thought I must have banged my head against the wall while I was turning in my sleep. Then in the course of perhaps half an hour it had grown worse until my whole head, neck and face seemed to be splitting apart. I thought my head would explode, literally. It went on and on and on, a steady, unbearable ache. Lying still didn't help. I reproached her for not giving me pain killers, and she was very contrite. She said it was important for the experimentation to run its course, and she promised me it would not happen again.

"A terrible thing was done to me next. Ivan, who I considered my friend, took me to a soccer field on the island. He told me to jog with him. I told him he was crazy, I was far too weak. He said, 'These are doctors' orders. For your own good. They know what they are doing, and they are the best in the world. They will cure you.' I began to jog. Ivan jogged by my side. I was still wearing smock and slippers, and must have looked ridiculous to the guards in the radar towers. As soon as I started to run I got vertigo. I was reeling, not jogging. I begged Ivan to let me stop but he told me to keep going, and took my arm. I don't know whether he was running faster, or if it was my imagination. Perspiration poured off me. The last thing I remember, to my horror, was the awful headache returning, and then I collapsed unconscious. What happened immediately afterwards I do not know.

"I was allowed to rest a few days. The headache went away, and I felt reasonably good. I ate my meals. I had plenty of time for thought, and the truth suddenly dawned on me. I was not being experimented on for radiation sickness at all. Hell, I had been working in the mines for years. I had seen comrades go down with radiation sickness. I knew the symptoms. I knew how they were treated.

"I was being treated and experimented on for something completely different.

"The experiments continued. The doctors seemed to be less friendly, and I started to get the impression that they were suffering from bad conscience. I began to go blind, and debilitated. I had to be carried by Ivan and another orderly to the bathroom, and to the surgery where I was treated.

"It seemed these symptoms were just what they were working at, and they lost all interest in me. I was put in a smaller, less comfortable room, and abandoned. I thought they were leaving me to die. I am sure even now that they had acquired fresh human material from the mainland, different skins to prick, and so on.

"Except I didn't die. I have to be strong to have lived the life I have, a prisoner and a miner since I was a kid. I began to get better. I could walk by myself. My blindness continued to the extent that my eyesight was badly impaired, and I was fitted for glasses by the senior doctor. I wandered around the island, quite freely because it was impossible to escape. I even kicked a ball around with the soldiers.

"Then, suddenly my symptoms returned even worse than before. The doctors told me that they had failed and that I would soon die."

XVII
Munich
West Germany

McDonald was not allowed to leave the house until it was time to go to the airport at Munich —forty-five minutes away. He passed the time alone with Ernst in a front room. Ernst was a highly educated man and they talked of many things.

Sometime during the late evening they were told that the sick man had passed away. Neither man said anything, but both knew how close it had been.

In the early morning they left for Munich Airport. Ernst and McDonald were in the back seat of the car. McDonald was exhausted, but he found he couldn't nap, as he had hoped. He was thinking of Saul, and wondering if he should try again with this sympathetic and understanding man.

Ernst read his silence. "Something is bothering you. Perhaps I could help."

McDonald said, "I do need help, but it concerns another matter. Strictly personal. I am reluctant to trespass on your kindness."

Ernst smiled, a smile that creased his face in deep, humorous lines. He took out a corncob pipe. "I have the time. I would welcome a change of subject myself."

McDonald took out the picture of Saul from his

briefcase. Ernst was such a first-rate fellow, McDonald was almost tempted to tell him the whole story.

"One of your people told me that he is dead. Somehow, I can't believe it. Maybe because I don't want to. It is important for me to find him. It has something to do with the death of President John Kennedy."

Ernst studied the photograph as he puffed his pipe alight. "I know him."

McDonald suddenly ceased to breathe.

"He is a mercenary. I think he is a native of Poland. If he had anything to do with the death of your President, there is only one role he could have played."

McDonald's voice reflected his excitement. "Do you know where he is?"

"No. But I have seen him since the death of your President. Here is something that might interest you. I thought little about it at the time. Indeed, only when you yourself mentioned the President just now, does it become significant. Some months before President Kennedy was killed, an inquiry was being circulated about this man. Someone wanted to contact him. Word went out that someone needed his services."

"Can you remember when you last saw him, and where it was?"

Ernst puffed and looked out at the countryside. "Spring," he said. "A year back. I was taking some information to Oslo, Norway. Somehow he was connected. We talked for a few minutes. I had the feeling business was not good. His shoes were down at heel. A deadly man, but one I felt I could trust."

"Trust?" McDonald knew what Ernst meant,

but the word sounded odd in the context of a professional assassin.

"As I trust you, and you trust me. In our business, if it is discovered we are not to be trusted, we finish belly-up in some river. Do you not agree?"

"As a matter of fact, I do. I trust the man, oddly enough. And in a strange way, I believe he would me. Did he have a name?"

"No. We identified with a four-phase recognition plan. I do not know your name, either, nor you mine. What a question!"

McDonald was now more excited than he had been since Herman Kimsey told him the original story in Dallas. He leaned forward. "I have a mental code name for him, Ernst. I call him Saul. Could you find him for me? Please. This is a personal mission. Whether or not you say yes, I will keep on trying."

Ernst nodded, reflectively, as though he were engaged in a conference with himself. "I think so, but I am not sure I would be permitted. Would you? Suppose I came to you for help in some matter, and then introduced a mission completely different, would you put the services of your group at my disposition?"

A good point. "It would depend."

"President Kennedy is dead. You cannot bring him back to life, and there is so much to do today. Tomorrow. I am more concerned with the flower of Soviet intellectualism locked up in insane asylums. I am more concerned with Czech freedom crushed, Hungarians massacred, East Germans imprisoned inside a shroud of steel slivers."

McDonald said, "Believe it or not, I have no animus to this man, any more than I would for a runaway truck that might have killed the President. In a strange way, Ernst, I almost identify with him. I keep thinking, I am old enough to be his father. My hate is for whoever hired his trigger finger. These sons-of-bitches who are above the law, who kill whoever stands in the way . . ."

"I will do what I can," Ernst said. "If anything develops, I will contact you through regular channels. I promise you nothing, but . . ."

"But?"

"You may get a surprise. Whether it will be a pleasant surprise or an unpleasant surprise is for you to decide."

Saul lived!

Saul was around. He had been pinpointed to Oslo, Norway within the last year. McDonald wanted to cheer. He was convinced that Ernst intended to help him. The man was cultured, sensitive and sympathetic. And he was intrigued. The life of espionage, like that of a cop, was mostly boredom. Suddenly Ernst found himself an integral part in history's most shattering assassination since that of Julius Caesar. Ernst would deliver the goods, in one form or another, if he could. And, more than that, for the first time, the man of violence in Washington, D.C. had a name that would run the length and breadth of the international underground.

Saul.

The full understanding of what lay ahead made his stomach knot, as if he were rushing at full speed down the Cresta Run. What it meant was that, somewhere, Saul would be waiting for Hugh C. McDonald to arrive.

101

XVIII
Washington, D.C.
The Central Intelligence Agency

And then . . . nothing.

In London, he was contacted and given some further material on the frightening experiments on Vozrozdenya. Blue Fox had no further instructions for him. Any delay in his return to Washington would be a betrayal of the people who were paying him. He told his contact he was on his way to Amsterdam for an overnight stay at the Hotel Doelen, and would leave for the United States the following day from Schiphol Airport. KLM. At 11:45 A.M. The organization had every detail of his movements should it seek to get in touch with him.

It didn't.

In Washington, McDonald checked in at the Statler Hilton to prepare his report. He was finished by early evening, and decided to call Herman Kimsey for dinner. An answering service told him that Kimsey was temporarily out of town.

McDonald was just as glad. He ordered up a rare roast beef sandwich and a glass of milk. He was feeling drained and exhausted. And tomorrow would be a tiring session.

It was more than tiring. It was totally frustrating. His CIA contacts received his report with smiling affability, and an indifference that seemed to McDonald to verge on the criminal. After hours of fruitless argument, he realized he was getting the old "Don't call us—we'll call you" treatment. The best he could do was a promise from the last man he talked to that his report would be bucked upstairs to the Director's office as soon as it was thoroughly analyzed. McDonald returned to the Statler seething—and puzzled.

The next morning he asked for, and got, an appointment with a Senator he had known for years. He hoped that, when his friend heard the story, he might be able to ask enough embarrassing questions to get the CIA off its collective ass.

McDonald knew that his report was classified, and that he was breaking security in the most flagrant way—but he was too mad to give a damn.

What the Senator told him made him even madder.

"I think you're stymied, Hugh. We seem to be going through one of our 'Let's be friends with Russia' periods. In confidence, I'll tell you that some big things are being planned. The word from upstairs is all 'Detente' now. Nobody wants to tickle the tiger. Maybe you should try the UN people. What you've told me is surely in their bailiwick."

"For Christ's sake," McDonald fumed, "if our own government won't scream about what I believe is a direct threat to the nation—what the hell could the UN do?"

McDonald was all the way back to California before he calmed down. He could only wait and hope that the CIA would grant his request to clear the Vozrozdenya report for publication.

It took a month, and even then he got only part

of the material released. But at least he was free to tell the story.*

McDonald immediately called Kimsey in Washington, to ask for his help in finding a publisher, and arranged to meet him for lunch the following week.

*The Hour of the Blue Fox, Pyramid Publications, 1975.

XIX
Washington, D.C.

McDonald was shocked at Kimsey's appearance. He had always been a heavy man. The clothes he wore were made for a heavy man, and his skeletal head seemed to disappear inside them. He took a handkerchief from what now seemed a cavernous pocket and mopped beads of sweat from his forehead.

Kimsey did not cultivate friends. He was essentially a loner. But McDonald believed that, insofar as Kimsey had friends, he, Hugh McDonald, was a friend. The two of them walked into the hotel restaurant, and Kimsey took Hugh's arm. "There comes a point," Kimsey said, "when time runs out."

With his shrimp cocktail, McDonald ordered a glass of dry Rhine wine, Kimsey nothing. He drank water. He said, "The doctors are putting me in the hospital next week for open-heart surgery. They tell me there's no other choice."

McDonald was appalled. He had faced death with this man more than once. He had always considered Herman Kimsey invulnerable to human weakness. He was something of a pain in the ass, yes. But he was as tough as teak.

"Hugh, I have an idea I won't leave the hospital alive."

Kimsey was too honest a man for pleasantries or false comfort. McDonald said, "Shit, Herman, I'm close to sixty myself. We all have to cross the line sometime. The exact place and date make no difference. One of the comforts is that we don't have to read our obituaries, or listen to the eulogies of our friends."

"You're right, Hugh. So what can I do. My impending demise makes me want to be useful."

McDonald felt an overwhelming sadness, and a sudden sense of his own mortality. He obviously couldn't ask for the help he had hoped for from this gravely ill man.

"A few phone calls should do it—to anyone you know who might be interested in publishing the Vozrozdenya story. I'm determined to get it before the public."

"Of course," Kimsey said, "I'll do what I can."

McDonald hesitated. "There's one other thing . . ."

Kimsey grinned at him. "Last chance for questions? Is that it, Hugh?"

Embarrassed, McDonald said, "Something like that, I suppose.

"I need reassurance, too. I am very depressed. Confirm for me the story you told me during the Goldwater campaign in Dallas, six years ago."

Kimsey looked directly into McDonald's eyes. People who understand animals say they seldom look at each other eye-to-eye because the posture represents a challenge to fight. Weak as Kimsey was, his glare was unblinking and unmistakable. "I have told you once. Do you want me to repeat it? Why? For discrepancies? You won't find any. I have not forgotten a word the bastard told me."

McDonald shook his head, and adjusted his

glasses to observe the consistency of the steak he had ordered. He said, "I am going to blow the story to the public, and I want confirmation, not from you, but from the man I met in your office. I've got to find him."

"The man you call Saul."

Hugh McDonald smiled with bright white teeth, and tucked his napkin into his throat. "The man every agent in Europe now calls Saul."

Kimsey had ordered shredded wheat. He said, "They will kill you."

"They? Why *they*? Surely you mean *he*?"

Kimsey became very agitated, and McDonald was worried he might suffer a seizure. "Goddamnit, Hugh, why can't you leave it alone? Why keep pressing so hard? Just let the matter die."

"Not if I can help it."

"There's a perfectly sound and valid theory about the Kennedy assassination. Why can't you accept it?"

"I am all ears. But I believe only Saul."

"Lee Harvey Oswald did it."

"That's original. Try me some more."

"Listen, Hugh. The Russians let Oswald into the Soviet Union. Why? The guy's a psychopath. The Russians can recognize a psychopath as quickly as we can. The Russians are all psychopaths. They then let him marry a Soviet girl. Why? Usually they kick a foreigner out if he expresses any such intention. And this is no ordinary Soviet girl. She has a university degree. The Soviet Union has spent many years and a lot of money on her. She is a State investment. And then the KGB let them both out. *Both*. Hugh, Oswald was programmed to kill. Like a medium at a seance. Then the mechanism went on the blink, and Oswald became

107

a dangerous toy without direction, popping off at the wrong people, like General Walker and ultimately the President of the United States. That's what happened."

"Do you believe this?"

Kimsey sighed, and shrugged resignedly. "Jesus, you're a stubborn bastard." He looked ineffably weary.

"After I'm dead, say what you like. I cannot help you contact Saul, because I haven't the strength or energy. But listen to me, Hugh, for your own good. I believe there are certain private interests involved who will destroy you, if you keep on. They may not kill you. They will try to ruin your reputation and your credibility. You are now a private businessman. Suddenly you will find yourself with no customers. Suddenly you will get unexpected income tax audits. The CIA and FBI will not use you any more. A helicopter you fly will crash, and alcohol found on your breath—heroin and LSD in your apartment. Some babe you lay will accuse you of rape. Any or all of these things will happen. Take my word for it. If you still persist, they will . . . eliminate you. They have too much at stake to let you run around loose. That's what I believe. And you better believe it, too."

The words were chilling. Hugh McDonald knew his man, and knew the depths of his contacts. "Who are these people, Herman? What you seem to be saying is that you know even more about the assassination of Kennedy than what Saul told you."

Kimsey sweated some more, and said, hoarsely, "I know that the scheme which Saul described could not possibly have been activated successfully without help from very high places in this country. It isn't Saul you are taking on, Hugh. Forget Saul. The threat from him could be removed damn fast. You could kill him before he could kill you. But the other people . . . hell . . . you don't even know who they are. They could be employing me, for all you know. And I wouldn't know who they were, either."

McDonald called for the check.

"I am going to find out, Herman, somehow. After Saul's story comes out, these invisible people will have to make a move."

"And then?"

McDonald cocked his head to one side, quizzically. "Then we will know who they are. Right?"

Kimsey did not immediately reply. A waitress came with the check, and went away with money and a tip. He then said, "OK, I'll make a deal with you. I don't want to die, but if I do, you have my permission to use Saul's story. You will find confirmation in my effects, dates and appointments in my diaries and so forth. Leonard Davidove will have them. Ask him to let you go through them. You will spot anything that may be relevant to Saul. Except his name. That's *your* invention."

The two walked out of the restaurant, through the lobby of the Statler Hilton. McDonald held Kimsey's arm and stopped him. "One question, Herman. A question which might change everything we have talked about."

"Hugh, I'm too sick to care. Shoot."

"Do you really believe Saul's story? Are you convinced he told you the truth, that he isn't some kook? If he *is* a kook, I have already made a horse's

109

ass of myself, and I don't want to make myself a bigger one."

Kimsey lifted his hand for a taxi, and said, "He told me the truth, Hugh. He shot Kennedy. I knew he shot Kennedy even before he talked to me. You will have a hell of a time proving it. But it can be done."

Herman Kimsey died three weeks later.*

In Los Angeles, McDonald got the news through a telephone call from Len Davidove.

"I was at the graveside," Davidove said. "I never saw so many VIP's. You'd have been proud of him, Hugh."

Belatedly, through his grief, McDonald asked, "What about his papers, Len? He wanted me to have them."

"Are you kidding? Hugh, I've been in business in this city all my life—and I never saw anything like it. They didn't even wait for the poor bastard to die. The Company, the FBI and every other intelligence agency in town was all over his place like a colony of ants.

"And you know, Hugh, it's a funny thing. Fifty-five years of living—and they got it all into one medium-sized briefcase."

McDonald hung up in sadness, and with an odd sense of relief. At that moment he decided to give it all up. He told himself that a man had to know when he was licked.

---

*Some very important people attended Herman Kimsey's funeral. This seemingly anonymous, unassuming man was a Knight of St. John of Jerusalem (Malta) and decorated by many nations for his services. Dr. Sayer of the National Cathedral, who has conducted services at the funerals of three Presidents, read the eulogy for Herman Kimsey.

XX
London
Winter, 1972

For eighteen months, Hugh McDonald worked for his company, World Associates, flying his helicopters, seeing old friends in the various police departments.

Then one day he received a telephone call from New York. By the familiar code phrase, the caller identified himself as belonging to Blue Fox. He said, "I have been asked to tell you that we have made progress in locating the person you are seeking. Are you free to return to Zurich?"

McDonald, his ear to the receiver, all his good intentions forgotten, was thumbing his address book for the number of his travel agent. "Register me at the Eden au Lac."

He allowed himself more than a month to wind up essential business, to brief his associates, and make his plans. This time he took the typescript of Herman Kimsey's statement on Saul from the safe deposit box. He had a certain intuitive feeling that at last it would be useful.

The following sequence can be told only in Hugh McDonald's own words:

"The airplane landed at Heathrow Airport some time after ten o'clock at night. I was dead tired and in a hurry to get to my hotel. What a joy are the British Customs! One goes in and out in a minute, and almost immediately I found myself at the taxi entrance, and the long line of waiting black taxis. I have spent so much time in London it is almost my second home, and I consider I know it almost as well as I know Los Angeles.

"Something happened now that had never happened to me before. Furthermore, checking with English friends, they agreed they had never had any such experience either.

"Before I got to the door, a young fellow approached me, and almost before he spoke, he began to take the bag out of my hand. If I had not been weary from jet-lag, I would probably have said something like, 'Hey, what's going on around here?', but I *was* tired, and he was pretty smooth. He was dressed in black with a white shirt, and I simply presumed he was my taxi-driver. I followed him across the street to a car which, although black, was not a London taxi-cab. Very quickly, he opened the trunk of the car, put my bag inside, then walked round and opened the door. The front door.

"I was still feeling vague. I thought it might be a hotel service. I remember times, before mass air travel, when uniformed men would be waiting with the words 'Claridges,' or 'Dorchester' on their caps. Then, thank the Lord, someone interfered. A regular taxi man, first in line, opened his door and came rushing over, and spoke to me. He said, 'Are you looking for a taxi, mister?"

" 'Yes. I have been picked up. Is there something wrong?'

" 'You bet there's something wrong, guv. This bloke's no cabby.'

"The driver who had taken my bags was small, perhaps five feet five inches, and spoke with an Irish accent. The taxi driver was not much bigger. The taxi driver said, 'What the bleeding hell's your game, mate? What are you trying to pull off? Piss off, or I'll stick you one.'

"I was completely bewildered. And then the Irishman got ugly. He said, 'Piss off yourself, you bastard. This man is my fare and I'm taking him into town.'

"The taxi-driver turned to me and said, 'Mister, I don't know what's going on, but this is a rip-off. This isn't a taxi.'

"Now I was beginning to think clearly. Hell, I'm a cop, and I know a hi-jack when I see one. I told the phony to get my bag out and blow. Almost simultaneously the two men went for each other with fists. Thank heaven, before I could join in on the side of the cabby, the constable on duty at the entrance saw the fracas, and walked toward us, not fast because in private disputes, haste is counterproductive; everyone might decide to turn on the cop. The phony driver saw him coming, rushed to the trunk, opened it, threw my bag on to the toes of the taxi-driver. He slammed the trunk down, ran to the driver's seat and drove off.

"In a few minutes, I was settled comfortably, except for a heart full of butterflies on the thruway to London. London taxi-drivers are not loquacious like New York cabbies. They would rather drive than talk. But this one could not get over the incident, and kept half-turning back through the compartment window. He said, 'Guv'nor, I've been driving cabs back and forth between Heathrow and the West End ever since I got out of the Forces six years ago, and I've never seen anything like that in my life. The *nerve!* With all the licensed cabs lined up across the road!'

"I was thinking it over. It couldn't be Saul's work. Yet it was planned. The guy was not looking for the first patsy coming out of Customs. He was waiting for *me.* I mean to say, for God's sake, if someone is simply hi-jacking, the last person a five-foot-five punk would want to grab would be me!

"You remember the attempt on my life in the hotel room at Garmisch. Then I was working on the Vozrozdenya case. But now there was a difference. I was here for one reason only: Saul. If this were a novel, I would provide an answer, but I can't. Was this guy acting for Saul, seeking to take me to Saul? I was scared.

"This latest incident seemed to me to be just one too many. In Garmisch and Augsburg my life had been threatened, and in one case I missed death by a razor's edge. But then there was another case I had simply dismissed as a crazy driver driving too fast. I had just stepped off the curb when this car roared round the corner, and believe me if I hadn't been on my toes and jumped back on to the sidewalk, I would, sure as Hell, have become a flatfoot. In Augsburg too —again I thought an accident—I was standing looking out of the window into a sort of court-yard. Something attracted my attention—a movement; what it was I can't recollect for the shock of what happened next. At that instant something fell from the roof. At first I thought it was somebody committing suicide. It was not. It was part of a shutter from a top floor slicing through the air like a knife. It missed my head by inches. It would have creamed me.

"I decided to call my old buddy at Scotland Yard, Deputy Assistant Commissioner of Crime retired, John Du Rose. I decided something futher, for no reason other than this incident. I wanted him to read the Herman Kimsey typescript on Saul. I wanted his comment, and his knowledge. If anything happened to me, Du Rose would get the message instantly and he would never let the case go. He would chase it to the end."

They dined first. McDonald recalls madrilene en gelee, a Welsh lamb chop with fresh peas, new potatoes and mint sauce, and a creme caramele. By that time it was closing time, 11:00 p.m., so they retired to the Polo Lounge, reserved for residents, and where, if they wished, they could drink all night. They sat in a corner. John Du Rose ordered port, McDonald, Courvoisier. Du Rose took the bound manuscript and started to read.

Half an hour later, Du Rose handed the manuscript back without a word. He looked into space, his bushy eyebrows contracted in a thoughtful scowl. McDonald remained silent for as long as his overpowering curiosity would permit. Du Rose sat in a low armchair. He wore a double-breasted suit and the lapel crinkled up to his chin. It came from a tailor who McDonald decided was not as good as his own.

McDonald finally exploded. "Well?"

Du Rose's reply was brief and to the point: Saul should be found, extradited, jailed, and tried for murder.

Hugh McDonald left for Zurich the next day and checked in at the Eden au Lac. He had not long to wait. Shortly before seven that evening, he had a telephone call from the same lady he had met on his previous visit. She was phoning from the lobby of the hotel, and suggested they meet in the bar. McDonald went to the bathroom, ran his electric razor over his evening shadow and hurried to the elevator.

Over Scotch and soda in the dimly lit cocktail bar she said, "I thought a great deal about the request you made last time we met. I confess I was very angry with you. I really meant it when I told you to finish the assignment you came for. I told you to leave us out of your personal vendettas. You didn't follow my advice, and I became angrier. With every contact you made, you inquired about Saul . . .

"But then, I said to myself, why not. We do not turn our friends down. You would do the same for us. We just want things done in their proper place and time."

McDonald remembers that as he listened to her voice, he felt a deep satisfaction that the name Saul was now well and truly pinned on the man he sought.

"I couldn't take your advice. I had to proceed. I am pleased that my breaking of the rules did not deter you from being helpful."

She said, "It has been difficult to pinpoint the man. Several of our people believe they know him. But without a name, it is not easy." She gave a quizzical laugh. "We call him Saul. Everybody calls him Saul except Saul, who doesn't know he is called Saul. The picture you left is not a good one. We do know, however, that he is a professional killer, which narrows the field. There are several such men, and we cannot be sure which is your man. There was a period of time when Russia trained teams of assassins in the Ukraine. One or two broke away and became free lance. If you saw him, would you recognize him?"

Although he had seen the man in the flesh for no more than thirty seconds, almost ten years before, McDonald had put that face together with the Identi-Kit a hundred times. My God! Would he know him!

All he could do was nod.

"That is good. We think then that it will be necessary for you to look at several men, and get to Saul by elimination. That is why we called you all the way across the Atlantic to Zurich. A man has arrived in this city who may be Saul. He is a killer. He is meeting two Arabs. It will be possible for you to observe him. He looks like the man in the picture."

McDonald could not believe that it could be so easy. His voice reflected his tension. "Can you arrange a meeting?"

In an almost teasing way she prodded his nose with her index finger. "One step at a time. A meeting, an actual tete-a-tete, would be very difficult.

117

There has to be some reason for him to talk to you. Let us observe him first. Perhaps a meeting will come naturally."

"So what is the plan?"

"We know he's taking a plane to Cairo from Zurich Airport tomorrow morning. We will arrange it so you have a good view of him . . ."

"View! I am going to take the plane myself, sit next to him!"

"You will do nothing of the sort. That would embarrass us a great deal. If the man *is* Saul, do not worry. He won't elude us."

She finished her drink and rose. McDonald rose with her, but she placed a hand on his shoulder, pressing him down. "Please stay there," she said. "I can find my way out. Maybe you had better have another drink. It may calm you down."

"Does it show that badly? No more drinks for me. I want to be totally alert tomorrow morning."

He remained over the dregs of his drink after she had left. In his mind's eye he recalled the slight hunch of the man's posture, the prominent nose, the thick, short hair now probably thinning and perhaps graying, the way he balanced on the balls of his feet, hands clenched.

Oh yes. He would recognize him.

It was a bright, clear day. Hugh McDonald welcomed it as though he were in training for a fight. He rose at 5:30. He did push-ups. He took a long walk before breakfast, breathing deeply. He showered, breakfasted on orange juice, coffee and croissants. Outside, the Zurich Sea was like glass, save where the famous Zurich swans bobbed like large balls of snow-white cotton.

That stage of violence, on Dealey Plaza in Dallas, seemed a million years removed from peaceful Switzerland of 1972, and even more from the cyclonic entry and exit of Saul in Herman Kimsey's office in the spring of 1961.

Could he be sure? Could those thirty seconds, the endless study of the photograph, the hours with the Identi-Kit, the words of Saul sprouting from the lips of Herman Kimsey, have accumulated into a composite fake? Did he exist? Did he have a wife? Kimsey was dead. Had Blue Fox, that brilliant and courageous organization, been persuaded by Hugh C. McDonald to waste its energy and prejudice its existence on a cruel wild goose chase?

In his statement to Kimsey, Saul said he often used a limp as part of his disguises.

Suppose the man at the airport was Saul but had given himself a completely different appearance since . . . yesterday.

After breakfast, McDonald paced up and down in front of the hotel, waiting for his contact to pick him up. At eight thirty, almost to the second, she double-parked her Fiat 124 in front of the hotel. McDonald hurried into the front seat, and she moved along with the thick lines of traffic that seem to snarl every city in Switzerland.

At a red stop-light, she said, "We want to be very careful that we don't influence you in any way. You must pick the man out for yourself."

"Quite."

"I'm glad you agree. I will take you to a certain place in the Airport Terminal. I will leave you there, alone. The man who may be Saul will arrive at the check-in window you will be watching. I will be watching from another location. If you positively identify the man as Saul, we will proceed from there."

McDonald's reply was somewhat resentful. "You are putting me to the test. I had hoped you would point him out to me, and that something about his appearance might trigger certain recognition factors."

She shook her head. "No. We decided against it. It's up to you. If it's not the man you seek, we will try again, until we run out of possibilities."

They drove in silence on the forty-minute trip to the airport, parked the car and entered the domestic section of the terminal where there was no Customs and Immigration clearance. The woman checked the watch on her wrist and said, "Keep your eye on the window just to your left. It shows flight number 725. That is the window where he will check in. It is now nine thirty. Watch very closely."

Before he could answer she had turned her back and hurried away. People began to arrive at the ticket window, people alone, couples, families. No Saul.

McDonald waited. The minutes passed. The time was nine forty five. He lit a cigarette, stubbed it out.

Then he saw something. Four men appeared together. Three were swarthy, Arabic-looking, two wearing drooping Taras Bulba moustaches. One had a blunt, Slavic face with a broad-tipped nose, about forty. The last was in a hurry, impatient, as though the people ahead of him should give way to him. He carried a single piece of hand luggage, blue, without markings. His hair was a dirty blond and cropped short.

Saul.

Or was it?

McDonald felt sick with frustration. He could

not be sure. The man seemed to be almost urging the line to move faster. The resemblance to the Saul that existed in his own mental Identi-Kit was strong. But the image in his brain was not slipping into the mental overlay. It was maddening. The image was a blur.

He reached the window. While the girl at the counter was tearing out the various-colored slips, the man turned and spoke to his companion. In German.

Kimsey had felt that Saul was a middle-European, so he probably grew up with German as a second language. McDonald moved closer, to perhaps ten feet, and studied the man without making any attempt to conceal himself. The man saw him, looked at him indifferently and continued to speak. McDonald's German was fluent, but his accent was foreign, and he could never have tried to pass himself off as a born German. This man's German was German-German. One of his companions turned to the others and spoke in Arabic. It was quite obvious that he was translating what had just been said in German.

McDonald's heart sank. Educated Arabs usually spoke English. Saul, Hugh McDonald's Saul, spoke English like an American. The man took the ticket, shook hands with his companions, and disappeared. McDonald lunged forward, and feigned casualness. He asked one of the Arabs, in English, "Do you have the time, please?"

The request was such an everyday one that the Arab did not pause to consider that there were clocks all over the terminal. He looked at his watch and said, in English, "Four minutes past ten."

"Thank you very much."

"You're welcome."

He walked slowly, reflectively, to the exit. The woman joined him. She said nothing, but looked at him for a word.

"No," said McDonald. The woman sighed.

On the way back to Zurich, she asked, "Can you stay? In Europe? I mean for a period of weeks."

"No, damn it. I have my helicopter business in California."

"You have come all this way, and put us to a great deal of trouble."

"I know, I'm sorry. Do you have other people I could look at?"

"Yes, but it will take four to five weeks for you to see the three others we have located. When can you return?"

McDonald thought the question over. He felt listless. The disappointment was deep, and once again he was tempted to abandon the quest completely. He had almost exhausted his own curiosity on the subject. But he couldn't. Too many good people had gone to too much trouble, cashed in on their capital of expertise and inside contact, and this capital could not be renewed. Every question asked, every favor given meant one less question and one less favor available in the future.

He said, "I can return in the spring. Then I will be prepared to spend all the necessary time to see the thing through."

Keeping her eyes on the road, the woman said, "All right. I will in London in May. On the fifteenth meet me at 1600 hours in the bar of the Piccadilly Hotel. Do you know it?"

McDonald smiled. "I know it."

At the Eden au Lac, he stepped out of the car, and she was gone without even a goodbye. Like so many people in the business of espionage and counter-espionage, there was something wraith-like about her. The moment she was gone one had the feeling that she did not exist.

McDonald returned to his hotel room, checked his passport and flight ticket. He was depressed to realize how bored he had become with Saul, how much he looked forward to getting back to serious business in California, how great the mental and psychological effort would be to bring him back to Europe in the spring. But he had started the ball rolling again, and he could not stop it.

XXII
London/Oslo/Helsinki
Copenhagen/London
Spring, 1972

Back at home, McDonald continued to wonder whether the wiser decision would be to forget the whole thing. A serious family problem arose. One of his children became ill, and required long and expensive medical treatment. He moved part of the family to Seville, Spain. The child fortunately responded well, and ultimately made a full recovery. But the financial strain was considerable.

Then, as often happens at the right moment, a ship came in and he suddenly had the cash in hand to keep his appointment in London.

It was raining when he left Los Angeles. The passengers were warned that the bad weather would continue across the country. Hugh McDonald, still in pursuit of his will o' the wisp, his Holy Grail, or perhaps still tilting at the windmill created by Herman Kimsey, his dead Sancho Panza, wondered gloomily whether it was an ill omen, a foreboding of future failure. He was not a gambling man. He liked sure things, as all cops like sure things. As he fastened his seat belt he was sure of only one thing, that the trip had better pay off for him. If not, his involvement with the Kennedy assassination was over.

Hugh McDonald, as a detective, had often

known frustration and disappointment, but nothing as agonizing as the run-around he was given in the following days. From London he was directed first to Oslo. Again arrangements were made for him to view a man who might be Saul. At 14:00 hours, he stood on the water-front scanning people at the ticket booth for the ferry boat to one of the northern islands. He remained there until the ferry left. His contact joined him and said, "The man we nailed took the boat. He is an assassin."

"Yup. But he ain't Saul."

McDonald flew to Helsinki. A fellow who looked roughly like Saul checked in at a certain hotel. But it was not Saul.

The next stop was Copenhagen. Here the suspected Saul did not show up at all. McDonald waited at the Nyhavn Hotel for three days, viewing local porn magazines for lack of anything else to do. He was then told to go back to London. The fellow the organization wanted him to see in Copenhagen had gone to London instead.

He flew to London, and waited two days until he was contacted by the lady from Zurich. She took him to the Dorchester Hotel in Park Lane, and the two sat in the lobby watching the revolving doors. Then suddenly, there he was. He came through the door, walked to the reservation desk and asked a question. He then seated himself on a sofa not twenty feet away.

At first McDonald was sure the man was Saul. Everything seemed to fit into place. The right age, clothing, even the physical attributes, the way he moved on the balls of his feet and held his head. But for some reason there was a doubt, and the doubt became plural. McDonald knew that he must hear that unforgettable voice. He rose, and walked over to the man.

"Excuse me, sir. But haven't we met somewhere? I have the strongest feeling that we should know each other. From Washington, D.C., perhaps?"

The man studied McDonald's face speculatively. His eyelashes fluttered. "I don't think so," he said. "But if you care to join me for a drink, perhaps we could . . . place each other."

The fruity voice and the inference were obvious. McDonald grabbed the woman, and left. "Surely you can do better than that!" he panted, his nerves shot.

The woman shrugged, "He's an assassin. I can assure you of that."

Outside, on Park Lane, the woman stopped. "Well, Hugh, that's the lot. We have no one else. I am disappointed, but we have failed."

McDonald felt sick. "There is *nothing* more you can do?"

Her hand touched him on the shoulder. "Keep your eyes and ears open. Keep trying. Hugh, most—not all—of our people believe the person you are looking for does not exist."

McDonald said, "I need a drink." He took her by the arm to the Red Lion pub behind the Dorchester. It was shortly after opening time, and almost empty. The floors smelled of Javel water, and fresh sandwiches were stacked behind glass cases. The woman ordered a gin and tonic, McDonald a Scotch and soda. They helped themselves to ice from an apple-shaped bucket.

"One contact," said McDonald, "suggested that Saul is dead."

126

The woman had clearly lost the last vestiges of interest in the search. She did not seek to disguise the boredom in her voice. "Anything's possible."

"So I may be seeking the dead?"

"Or the non-existent."

"Shit!"

"Quite."

"What are you going to do?"

"Tell our people to stop wasting their time."

McDonald said with genuine gratitude, "I don't know your name. But thanks. It goes without saying—if you need me, you know where to get me."

She finished her drink. "I am sorry. How long do you intend to remain in London?"

"I'll do some shopping tomorrow, then leave for the United States on Saturday if I can get a reservation. Weekend flights tend to get jammed."

Indifferently, she said, "If I hear anything before you leave, I'll phone you at the Westbury."

She left. McDonald followed her a few minutes later, walked along Charles Street to Berkeley Square, across Bond Street to the Westbury. He gave a wave to Tony Sinclair, the society tailor across the street, an old friend. He picked up an early edition of the Evening Standard and took the key to his room. He sat there for several hours. He had forgotten lunch. And oddly enough, he had forgotten Saul. It had become a wasted and costly episode in his life. McDonald was not one for crying over spilled milk. Life was too short, and there was always so much to do.

By evening he was hungry and dined alone in the hotel. Afterwards he ordered brandy. When he heard his name being paged, he looked at his Patek watch, and realized to his surprise that it was eleven in the evening. The lady on the telephone said, "Hugh."

"Yes . . . hello."

"Are you all right? You sound funny."

"I'm fine."

"Remain in London. Day after tomorrow, you will be contacted at the hotel. Sit in the lobby between two and four in the afternoon."

"I have run out of cash. I am eating my credit cards."

The voice was disinterested. "It's up to you."

"O.K. Tell them I'll be there."

XXIII
Chicago, 1971

In a way, the ultimate confrontation between Hugh McDonald and Saul would seem to have about it a certain sense of destiny, as if it were preordained. International conspiracy is one of the facts of McDonald's life. If he does not find it, it tends to find him.

Some years ago, in 1970 and 1971, the general community of the United States was alarmed at a spate of random killings of policemen. The lives of cops are always laid on the line in the process of law enforcement. But this was something different. Just to be wearing blue was enough to be the target of some wanton sniper. Was it hate? Seasonal craziness? Or conspiracy?

McDonald was drawn into the case in Chicago, when he was receiving a shoe-shine from a talkative kid who would not keep his mouth shut, and boasted he was used as a tip-off by a certain taxi driver. McDonald wanted to know more. The kid talked more. McDonald waited for an opportunity to pick up the cab.

He decided to give the cab driver money in advance. The driver told him of meetings held periodically in private houses in various parts of the city, and that he, the driver, was hired to shuttle back and forth from the airport to pick up passengers from Algiers.

McDonald, wary, asked, "Algerians?"

"No. Americans."

"Blacks?"

"Both."

"Irish? Like I.R.A.?"

"Hell, no. Some of the whites don't even speak English."

McDonald's curiosity was aroused with a vengeance. In the decade or so since Houari Boumedienne took over the Presidency from Ben Bella, he made Algeria one of the world's more secretive countries. Nobody today even knows if Boumedienne is married. He also offered hospitality to many dissident groups, some black, some Communist, militant students, the I.R.A., any who wanted to upset or overthrow society in the United States, Britain or West Germany (being frightened of General de Gaulle, he was careful to keep his hands off France).

The chance shoe-shine took McDonald to Canada, then London, Zurich, Spain and finally Algiers, where he holed up in the Hotel Aletti, and observed several houses in the residential area of El Biar which, during French rule, was almost totally European.

What he discovered, among many conspiracies, was a blueprint to disrupt and undermine the effectiveness of American law enforcement agencies. The relationship between civilian and policeman is always a delicate one. A man with a gun is always at a psychological distance from a man without. If the police can be made jittery, they will see enemies everywhere, especially in black, Hispanic or radical student communities.

The conspiracy included a plan by which it was careful *not* to form an obvious pattern. The killers were to slaughter in different cities, and in different ways.

The more wanton the killings, the more militant would the police become, out of the necessity to stay alive. The more militant and savage the police became, the more distasteful they would become to the public. Thus the Algerian cop-killing mission would be successfully accomplished. The civilized relationship between that of law and that of order would be disastrously undermined.

McDonald found, to his dismay, that much of the financing for the conspiracy was being supplied by "good Americans," liberals who believed they were helping civil rights, who were outraged that people were forced out of the United States by injustice, the Viet Nam war, drug persecution, racial oppression. These people fought the "good fight" for the Rap Browns, the Angela Davises and the Eldridge Cleavers of the protest movements. They gave their money in great gobs to sympathetic organizations—and the money found its inexorable way to the training camps of Algeria. Fifth Avenue radical chic money, raised with the best of intentions, was being used to kill cops on the beat—and the occasional politician or government official.

He found that the Algerian Government asked no questions. Its only proviso was that the Government itself was not to be implicated or embarrassed. Valuable foreign currency was coming into the almost derelict country. China, too, was funneling money into the group, and Algeria wanted to stay on good terms with China.

Those running the Algerian operation, mostly

black American defectors, recruited footloose, tough young men from all over the world. It was important that they had to be free of any kind of police record, either local or international. No known crooks need apply. The last person the police of St. Louis, Missouri would suspect, trying to track down the motiveless murder of one of their number would be, say, a Swedish, or Scottish, or, for that matter, a Seattle tourist in town for a day or two.

A very precise price list was established by the group (these killers, it must be remembered, were fundamentally amateurs to be used once only; a professional like Saul dictated his own price to a large degree). A city, county, state or Federal policeman would bring the killer $5,000 in cash. State politicians, exclusive of Governors, were worth $7,000. A Governor was worth $10,000 or more, depending on his importance, charisma, and Presidential potential. Democrats were always worth more than Republicans, for obvious reasons. Republicans tend to have more money and so see little of the police. Democrats brush more closely with them so the basis for anger and abrasion is much stronger.

Some key political figures were worth $20,000. The attempt on the life of Senator John C. Stennis of Mississippi in 1973 would have been worth $20,000. Money was doubtless still paid over because of its disruptive effect.

The paid killers did not have to visit the Algiers GHQ. They could be recruited anywhere. McDonald is convinced that William Bremer, the twenty-one-year-old attempted assassin of Governor Wallace of Alabama in 1972, was hired by the Algiers group. Wallace himself has puzzled openly how a young punk "earning a busboy's wages"—Wallace's own words—could travel through America and Europe, renting cars.

"Target Blue" was a frightening new fact of American life throughout 1973. It shook police morale badly, but the morale held, and there were few incidents of panic, or irresponsible counter-shooting.

Target Blue then died away so abruptly that the fact of conspiracy was, by definition, established. General, uncoordinated emotions just don't come and go that way. The killers had been ordered off.

Neither McDonald nor the police in general claim credit for the cease-fire. What happened was that the Algerian government was burning its own fingers. It found its sinister guests too fierce for comfort and expelled almost all of them. They have not yet re-assembled, and for good reason. Where can they go? There are not many available countries to go to.

Libya would admit them happily, but what Irish patriot wants to conspire in a country where he can't have a drink? Idi Amin, the fat clown of Uganda, would welcome them, but American blacks are almost inevitably outraged by the way they are treated in black Africa. Castro got fed up with conspirators years ago, and rooted them out. In the Soviet Union and China they would have to toe the Party Line. Allende's Chile might have been ideal, but Allende was killed.

So America, and America's policemen can breathe again—for the time being.

XXIV
June, 1972
London, England

McDonald sat in the furthest corner of the lobby. He had told his contact exactly how to find him: enter lobby and turn right, then walk to the furthest corner of the lobby, where there was a nook with a long sofa and two overstuffed armchairs. He knew they would have plenty of privacy there. Then, after waiting an hour, two men came in, and looked around. One was a stranger.

The other was Saul. This time there was no question, no possibility of mistaken identity, the rough, tough face something like a younger George Wallace. From forty feet away, McDonald recognized him.

McDonald remained seated. Both men crossed the bar, diagonally, from the corner entrance to the opposite corner. The stranger spoke first. "This is the gentleman you wanted to meet. I have talked to him about you. He has been curious to meet *you* for a long time."

McDonald rose and the three men shook hands. The odd formality and politeness, the use of the word "gentleman" in connection with a professional killer, made him want to laugh, perhaps a little hysterically.

The murder business seemed to have served Saul well over the years. He was dressed casually and expensively—blue tweed jacket over a white shirt, open at the throat, darker blue doeskin slacks and Gucci loafers. His hair was still thick and short—but slightly gray at the temples.

"I'm glad you are curious, too," McDonald said. "Do you remember me? We have met."

Saul studied him for a moment, and then, in that low controlled voice which had chilled him eleven years earlier, "Yes. You are a friend of Herman Kimsey's. I saw you in his office after the Bay of Pigs. He and I discussed you several times after that."

The stranger interrupted. "I must leave now. I am glad I could bring you two together. *Adios.*" Neither McDonald nor Saul turned to see him go. The two sat down. Saul spoke first. "What do you want? I have been told that you might have work for me to do."

McDonald shook his head. "I was lying. You know, of course, that Herman is dead."

"What does that have to do with our business?

"Nothing. His death was unfortunate, and I'm sorry he is not here with us. You would probably have felt more at ease."

For at least two minutes Saul did not speak. Two minutes is a hell of a long time to remain under the scrutiny of a man like Saul. He said, "It doesn't matter. Kimsey was only a man I met occasionally in my work."

This was the opening which Detective Hugh McDonald was waiting for. He had written text-books and lectured innumerable times on the techniques of interrogation. One of his basic precepts was: "Get the subject to talk about anything,

135

and sooner or later he will talk to you about the subject you are interested in."

McDonald, choosing his words with great care, said, "If that is true, why did you tell him the story about your activity in our country . . . activity that has caused so many problems?" Hugh was avoiding names, places, dates, anything that could be counterattacked with a specific denial.

Saul said, "I told him nothing. What has this got to do with you? You have been looking for me for years."

McDonald now held the advantage of counterattack. "I was doing the lying before. You are doing the lying now. I have you pinned down, my friend. You told Herman everything, and I want to know why."

It is important to note that up until this moment, neither man had mentioned the Kennedy affair. The only other time they had met was just after the Bay of Pigs. The workings of Saul's mind should logically lead to the presumption that it was the Bay of Pigs in which McDonald was interested.

The man was absolutely still. The art of being absolutely motionless, like a waxwork in Madame Tussaud's, is not an easy one. McDonald himself was not capable of it. Saul expressed literally the cliché about not moving a muscle. Hugh, in turn, reacted with another cliché. He felt his hair standing on end. Saul, in the same low-keyed, lethal voice, said, "You haven't answered my question. What business is it of yours?"

"Confirmation. I know the answers."

"I told Kimsey, because he knew the rules of the game. You know the rules of the game, too. Tell this story to anyone else, and you won't survive on this earth another week."*

136

Saul talked quietly for an hour and forty five minutes. He was suddenly relaxed, almost friendly, man to man, two equals in the same trade. He talked not about the Bay of Pigs, but how he pulled the trigger that killed President Kennedy. McDonald seldom interrupted. The story had only minor discrepancies with the story Herman Kimsey had given in the summer of 1964. All loose ends were now tied up, all the mysteries of the assassination solved, all the contradictions reconciled.

Never before in McDonald's career had he felt such a necessity to test every word by all of the methods used by expert interrogators as he did while Saul was speaking. And McDonald was an expert. His book, *The Psychology of Police Interrogation,* is an American police standard. In the Army, in his 301 File, one of the areas of expertise checked is that of interrogation. McDonald says, "I had the feeling that Saul had gone over the story more than once. He must have talked about it to other people. His memory, after nine years, in my opinion, could not recall with such detail and fluidity. The oral statement he had given me was so very close to the statement I had made of Herman Kimsey's conversation that I have to assume he

---

*One of the questions most often asked is why did Saul talk about his activities with either Kimsey or McDonald. McDonald replies, "I think Saul answers that question himself when he says, 'I told Kimsey because he knew the rules of the game and you know the rules of the game, too.' " Like doctors discussing, on a purely professional basis, an intricate or new technique, Saul was talking to people he felt were professionally in the same business, or at least in a business closely akin to his specialty. In this context, Saul almost had to talk. After all, who kills the President, develops a new surgical technique, or breaks the bank at Monte Carlo, and never says a word about it?

had discussed the matter in detail with persons over the years. None of the attributes of the liar were visible as Saul talked. No white knuckles, no unusual hesitation, no emotional problems. It was an easy, self-assured statement of fact."

McDonald suggested the two should go up to his room. Saul was quite hoarse. "Why?"

"I have something to show you that will interest you."

"You have no thought of trying to detain me?"

"I wouldn't dare."

The man thought, and nodded. He obviously agreed. McDonald would not dare. They went into the room together. The bed had been made, and a packet of laundered shirts had been delivered. McDonald snapped open his briefcase, brought out an unmarked folder containing a long typescript. "I want you to read this . . ." he paused.

The man smiled, somewhat sardonically, "You can call me Saul. After all . . . you always have. It's the best you can do."

"I want you to read this, and correct it. Make any changes that you think will make it more factual."

He took it with his right hand, and, for the first time, Hugh McDonald felt as if he had taken a physical blow. Once again, he had shaken the hand that killed John F. Kennedy.

Saul settled down in an armchair, and almost immediately looked up, startled. All he said was, "Well, I'm damned." He repeated it several times as he read, and reading seemed almost to hypnotize him. He had never dreamed that the story had been written down. He made only one change. Kimsey had used the word "Mauser" when he described the gun that killed Kennedy. Saul said, "Not a Mauser. Change that to 'European rifle.' "

When he finished, he stood up to leave the room. He said, "You are crazy. Christ, I should hate to be in your shoes, owning that document."

"Why?"

"It's as good as a suicide note. It's a grenade with the pin pulled out. If I were you, I would regret the day you learned what you know. Guns will be trained on every move you make for the rest of your life."

One thing Saul had to know was that McDonald did not fear him. And, in truth, he was so dizzy with elation at the final triumph of his quest he did not know whether he was frightened of Saul or not. "Fair enough," he said.

"It took you years to find me," Saul went on. "And it will take you years to find me again. Yet I can have you watched day or night. Step out of line, and I have merely to pick up the phone and make one call. You'll never know what hit you."

They stared into each other's eyes, and a curious realization seemed to strike each simultaneously. What Saul had said was not a threat, but a warning, almost as from one friend to another. Yet again, as he had done periodically over the years, McDonald felt a disturbing sense of *alter ego,* that the two of them were in a way interchangeable. And in the end, it was he, Hugh McDonald, who was the hunted. From now on, Saul was the hunter.

Saul almost smiled. He thrust his hands into his pockets, lifted his shoulders as though stretching, lowered them again, turned on his heel and walked out of the room—cool, completely confident and at ease. The wages of death were . . .

Enormous.

XXV
Saul's Admission To Hugh C. McDonald in the Lobby of the Westbury Part I: The Set-Up

"Why Guatemala, you ask me? I was called to Guatemala for a gathering of mercenaries. They were being employed and paid by a group described as the 'Cuban Government in Exile.' A training ground, reasonably well equipped, had been established. There seemed to be plenty of money available to hire and train an invasion group. The group was small but trained on elitist, commando lines. The plan was to invade the island of Cuba at a place called the Bay of Pigs . . . then disengage as quickly as possible, infiltrate into the Sierra Maestra mountains, Castro's old battleground, and defeat Castro the same way Castro defeated Battista."

McDonald remembers his impatience. His neck muscles were rigid and a pain began to form behind his ear. The temptation to tell Saul to get on with it was overwhelming, but he knew that he must let Saul tell it his own way. No interruption must be allowed to stop the flow of this man's reminiscences. For that's what they were —battlefield stories of one old soldier to another. Later, when Saul was well into it—then, he could ask his questions.

"Basically, the operation was to force the attention of the world on the resistance to Castro. Secretly we hoped there would be no fighting at all, that the Cuban army and the Cuban people would flock to our side, and overthrow Castro in a *coup d'etat*. At least that's what we were told.

"I understood at the time that the United States Government was supporting the operation with money and equipment. We were paid in dollars. The equipment was American. I understood there would be an American military support for the invasion, followed by financial and logistic support once we reached the mountains and began a successful counter-revolutionary campaign. I was told clearly and plainly that the training camp was supported by 'an agency' of the United States Government, and that many of the instructors were provided by that agency. I had agreed to take part in the invasion and then to become a part of the training cadre that would remain in the mountain country of Cuba, the Sierra Maestra. Don't forget, our first purpose was to be disruptive wherever we could.

"During our training period in Guatemala— our morale was very high, incidentally; we were well fed, well treated, lots of broads in the district—a certain man would appear occasionally at the campsite. It was whispered around that he was one of the American agents. He seemed to be primarily involved in a type of industrial sabotage. Industrial sabotage is very important to a revolutionary effort. I never knew his name. You have called me 'Saul.' I called this guy 'Troit'. Detroit came up somewhere in conversation at the time, so I always thought of him as Troit."*

"I had no particular contact with Troit, certainly

---

*McDonald says, "This kind of vagueness is enormously convincing to a professional interrogator. If he had been more precise, I would have suspected he was embroidering, or doing some Monday-morning quarter-backing."

nothing officially. He seemed to find me pretty professional, which I was, and would seek me out from time to time. We talked. We had a few beers together. During our conversations he seemed particularly interested in the various methods that the modern assassin uses . . ."

At that point McDonald had a sudden devastating thought which chilled him. He decided to risk his first interruption. He felt he had to know the answer to one question—which might explain a lot. He hoped he could ask his question casually, without emphasis.

"Troit was not Herman Kimsey, by any chance?"

"No, I saw Kimsey only in Washington. I guess I met Troit not more than half a dozen times. Probably three or four hours altogether. It never occurred to me that I would meet Troit again, once the camp was abandoned, and the invasion was under way. Do you want me to tell you what happened on the Goddamned beach—and how I got off it?"

"No. That is part of history. I want you to get to the point." McDonald will never forget the quality of Saul's smile.

"Yes . . . I know you do. Well, sometime in the early spring of 1963, I began to get word from various sources, asking if I was available. I could only be available for one thing, so I was naturally interested. Certain people in Europe, North America and Latin America were letting it drop that I would be contacted—you know how that sort of thing is done by the way you chased me. I was not easy to find at the time. The fuck-up of the Bay of Pigs shook me up a lot, and I did a lot of travelling. I was in southern Europe, then South America, then Australia . . ."

"Working?"

"Yeah. One time I came back to the United States for a short period. I lived in Southern California for about a month, maybe six weeks, and then moved to Mexico. Business was good in Mexico, and that made it easy—or at least easier—to try to make contact with whoever was trying to make contact with me.

"The contact was finally established, but I could not activate a recognition factor . . . you know what I mean. I couldn't read the signals as to how to get in touch. I understood that one man only wanted to contact me, and he would not reveal his identity until he had a chance to observe me. From this I gathered he had met me before, but wanted to make absolutely sure that I was me, if you see what I mean. Just like you . . ."

"Just like me."

"You can understand my situation. The very nature of my business requires that I am constantly alert to any movement of persons who simply want to observe me. I never sleep in complete darkness . . ."

"Really?"

"I am damn sure there are a lot of people in this world who would like to observe me through the sights of a high-powered rifle. I guess it is because of the nature of my business that I feel the presence of being constantly hunted. You know the feeling as well as I do. It's not a bad feeling really. It's like being on a constant high, not that I would know, because I don't go for drugs. One lesson I have learned in life is that extrasensory perception is not necessarily something one is born with. One can learn it, sometimes the hard way. I have learned to depend on hunches, feelings, intuition and so on. You may not believe this, but I knew you were looking for me long before I was ever tipped off that you were . . ."

"I believe you. I know the feeling."

"After checking, very carefully, the circumstances surrounding this inquiry for me, I figured it posed no physical threat to me. The inquiries had the appearance of being 'open'—you know what I mean—circulating fairly frequently in the intelligence community. And by now they were really trying hard, so I played hard to get, to up my value for my special services. I could feel it was a big deal. By various means, this, that and the other, you know the moves, I let it be known I could be contacted in Haiti. This was acceptable to 'the man'. That was the only name by which I could identify the person I was supposed to meet.

"In the middle of May, 1963, I went to Haiti. I had been told to stay there for three days, within a certain geographical area . . ."

"Where?"

"The Hotel Ibolele, though I was supposed to be seen around Madame Rose's bordello."

"I know it well," McDonald smiled.

"During that time 'the man' would observe me, and if he recognized me as the person he was really looking for, he would approach me. The same story. Was I the guy he remembered? If he could *not* recognize me, or identify me as the person he had in mind for the job, he would deposit in the bank under an arranged name two thousand dollars which I could withdraw on the fourth day and go on about my business. No further sweat.

"It was during the second day in Port au Prince . . . at about four o'clock in the afternoon I received a telephone call. This was a bit funny in itself, because there were almost no telephones in service, thanks to Papa Doc, and the Ibolele could get the Pan American office and not much more. I was told to meet 'the man' at 7:30 that night at a private residence . . ."

"Did he really say 7:30?"

"No. Now you mention it, he said nineteen thirty, military fashion. I agreed, and precisely at that time, checking my watch, I knocked on the door of a pretty imposing residence. It seemed to me that whoever lived there had a lot of money, or some sort of official or governmental contact . . ."

"You could have checked that easily by seeing if there was a flagpole outside. That would have been an obvious clue."

"Why should I *want* to know? I'm just telling you as it happened. A young girl, Haitian, ushered me into a sitting room. She did not speak. She motioned me to follow her, as if she were expecting me. The room she took me to was furnished as a study, and the books that I could see were in English. It was a good room, a working room, dark paneled in Haitian mahogany. The drapes had been closed. There was very little light, only the one lamp on the desk. There was an air conditioner and it was pleasantly cool.

"From a publication I saw upside down on the large desk, I got the feeling that this place, the room, the house, had some sort of official connection. United States Government? I don't know. Don't ask me how, or ask me more, because I wouldn't be able to tell you. It was just my impression at the time, and I could have been wrong. It wasn't important at that time. You know as well as I how wise it is to know as little as possible.

"I was left alone for only a few moments, literally, perhaps ten or twenty seconds. The door opened and a gray-haired man walked in. I recognized him instantly . . ."

"Troit?"

"Right. The guy from the old days before the Bay of Pigs."

"What did he look like? Describe him."

McDonald remembers that Saul said nothing for what seemed an interminable time. His eyes held McDonald's without expression. McDonald had a sudden fear that he might have blown it with a question he should have had sense enough to know Saul would never answer. He realized he was holding his breath—and lit a cigarette as Saul began to talk again.

"In Guatemala we had spoken English and we used that language now. He was American, or I think he was American. His voice was friendly and easy, by which I mean there was no sense of pressure or urgency. It was like a friendly chat. He seemed very sure of himself, and very sure of me. This was unusual too, I mean for Chrissakes I could only be there for one reason! He spoke for a while about the old days, and then right out of the blue, he asked—get this straight —he asked me if I could be hired to kill the President of the United States."

McDonald said nothing. Saul did not pause.

"This man asked the question calmly, and with no dramatics. I almost fell over backwards in my chair. It was then I realized the important fact that he had made no attempt, either in Guatemala, or now, to introduce himself. As far as I was concerned he was Troit. By the same token, he didn't know my name either, only the phony name I used in Guatemala. I said I almost fell over, but I hoped I didn't show it, because if I looked scared, that

146

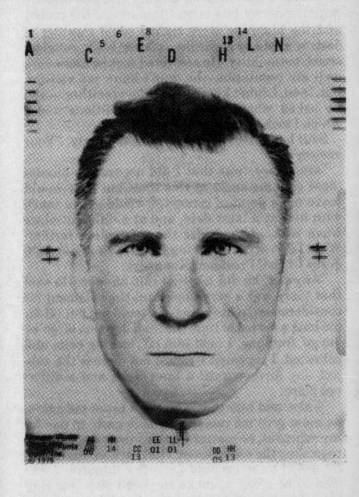

Identi-Kit Model II composite of Saul compiled by Hugh McDonald from memory of the 1972 meeting at the Westbury Hotel in London.

might have put the price down. I told him assassination was my business. I told him if the money and the planning were right I could contract to destroy anybody regardless of race, rank, religion, creed, nationality. He answered that he knew very well my reputation—he didn't know my victims, but, then, I didn't know my employers either!—and he asked what would be the conditions under which I took the assignment."

Saul hesitated. McDonald asked quietly, "Your answer?"

"My answer was that I did not care to discuss those circumstances at this time, but if he would leave me a point of contact, I would get in touch with him at a later date, and at a different place when we could consider the proposition further. What I was actually saying, I was saying to myself: Jesus Christ! President Kennedy!

"Anyway, he did not like this answer. He said that there was a very important time element for consideration in his plans. He could not put off for too long a period of time the final decision of 'go' or 'no go' from me. I held him off, looking calm and collected. I repeated I would not discuss the subject any further until a later time, and a different place.

"I also told him that if he were to see me again, he must give me two thousand in cash, to pay for my expenses, no matter what my decision would be regarding the assignment. His reaction was funny. He asked to be excused for a few minutes. I was glad to be alone to make my head stop spinning like a top. He was gone for—I guess—five minutes, long enough for me to feel a bit uneasy. On returning, he handed me twenty bills of one hundred dollars each, American, and said he would wait for not more than two weeks to be recontacted. If he did not hear from me after those two weeks, he would understand that I wanted no part of his plans. I knew that he had other assassins on his list, but preferred me, and I was flattered. He said he would meet me at any reasonable place in the world to discuss more detailed arrangements.

"I left the house. I did not even return to the Ibolele for my luggage. Shit, I had two grand in my pocket. I went directly to the airport. I took the first plane out, paying cash. It happened to be going to Buenos Aires.

"I stayed there for a week, at the Hotel Continental. I spent the time by myself going over everything I knew about Troit, because now it had become important that I be able to evaluate how authentic his offer was. I didn't want to know who was behind him. Just that Troit himself was reliable. It didn't add up to much. In Guatemala no one had ever actually *told* me he worked for the U.S. Everybody just accepted it that way—where most outsiders seemed to be from the CIA.

"It was there in Buenos Aires that I began to doubt that Troit was a United States Government man.

"I went over our meeting in Haiti. The house still seemed to me to have a sort of official atmosphere about it, sort of rich—but unlived in at the same time. Then there was the cash, produced so easily, without question. From his conversation it seemed he represented a group of people. He always said 'we', never 'I'. Of course this could be cover-up, but I rejected the idea. The project was so mind-blowing I couldn't believe that it could be the product of one person. Troit, I began to believe, represented a group with unlimited finances, who wanted John

149

F. Kennedy out of the way. I presumed they thought they could get out of the next President what they couldn't get out of Kennedy.

"I decided to go back to Guatemala. Troit and Guatemala were linked in my mind, and might give me a further clue. I set up the connection for Troit to meet me in that area. Eight days after the meeting in Haiti I was there. I made several discreet inquiries but could find no information on anyone who might be Troit. I was beginning to feel frustrated.

"After thirteen days, Troit appeared. We met in a hotel room, and got down to business right away. Troit was not quite the calm, relaxed fellow I saw in Haiti. He was tense. It was impossible to be otherwise when one is planning the assassination of the most powerful figure in the world. He not only appeared very nervous, but seemed to have some difficulty addressing himself to the problem. I thought I detected a sort of distrust in his attitude, wondered whether he was weaselling out. His attitude was catching. It began to make *me* nervous as well. I didn't know enough about him, and it worried me.

"I decided to bring the conversation to a point, or end it. I told him I was ready to proceed with any reasonable plan; that my price was fifty thousand dollars, half to be paid immediately and the other half to be deposited in a bank in Switzerland under a certain number when the contract was completed. This high price was a test in itself. I have worked for a lot less. I wanted to see just how serious he was, if the price would scare him off.

"He backed away from this one at first. He stated that the plans were still very indefinite, and that they were not yet ready to pay such a large sum of money. In fact, he said, the plan might be abandoned altogether.

"I stood up, and told him to shove it up his ass. I had understood, from the conversation, that the project had been firmed up, and was in the hiring stage. If that were not so, why in Christ's name had he contacted me in the first place, chasing me over two continents and then giving me two grand?"

"That *was* odd," McDonald said, and the very imprecision, he decided to himself, made it all the more believable. Real life does not slot in neatly, like a Christie or Forsythe novel. Amateurs were at work here, dealing with one professional.

"Troit changed his tune. He got very businesslike and assured me that the plans were firm, but that the time, date and place had not yet been selected. He then said something positive at last. The President must be assassinated in the year 1963. But other important details had not yet been clarified.

"I then told him that the most important part of the plot was being arranged right here and now —the hiring of the mechanic, the hit man, who would do the job and pull the trigger. If they were going ahead with the plot, they would have to hire the guy now. Troit paced up and down the room. He said the price was right but not the fifty per cent in cash on the barrelhead. I repeated what I had said before. Half in advance or no deal, mister.

"Then the businessman in him came up. If he paid me twenty-five thousand dollars out in front, how long would that bind me for? I told him he had answered the question himself. President Kennedy had to be killed in 1963. So the down payment bound my services until the first of January in 1964.

"He said nothing for quite a time, walked up and down, and then agreed. And then came the double-whammy, at least for me. He picked up a small traveling case, handed it to me, and told me to open it. I did so. It was full of money! I counted out twenty-five thousand dollars. There was a lot more in the case, and I dumped the rest on the bed. I replaced my twenty-five grand in the case and snapped it shut.

"Troit sat down, and with a gesture asked me to be seated, too. He told me the assassination would take place in Texas. Certain political and geographical conditions seemed to favor that location as the best place. What I figured was that Troit, or his people, had the *place* all picked out for the hit—but they didn't know yet how or when they could get the target there. That suited me fine. I could wait. Texas was close to the Mexican border. I could get in and out in no time at all. I agreed.

"He then told me something which, from what we all know today, is the most significant fact of all. He had a 'friend', a young man who had recently returned from the Soviet Union. This 'friend' was crazy enough to believe anything he told him. He said they had originally toyed with the idea of using the 'friend' as the assassin, but that the decision was abandoned because the guy was a nut, emotionally unstable. Troit then worked over the 'friend', convinced him that he, Troit, was working for the government. He told his 'friend' that the Government was very worried about the President's disregard of his own security. Troit's job was to find someone reliable to shoot some shots close to the President at some specified time and place. This would scare him into realizing how much he needed the Secret Service and better protective devices."

"What did you say?"

"I was listening. I realized he was outlining a ready-made plan, and he needed my approval. He went on talking. Several weeks earlier, he said, he had tested the idea by having this 'friend' fire some warning shots at a man who was embarrassing the Government. He told the 'friend' that he, the 'friend', would be paid by the CIA. His shots were to stop the man from annoying the Government. The 'friend' agreed and shot roughly in the direction of the man, who happened to be a retired general in the United States Army."

"General Walker."*

"Yeah. Troit said the kid did a good job and was given a hundred bucks in cash. The 'friend' thought he was working for the CIA and would jump at any chance of working for them again."

"Troit was speaking in pretty general terms, but I figured he was edging and backing toward a complete plan. I told him why the hell didn't he get to the point? He had invested twenty-seven thousand dollars in me. I reminded him assassination was my business, and whatever his plan was I was a pretty important part of it. He got huffy, and said there would be no more conversation that day. I shrugged my shoulders, put on my jacket and got ready to leave. He suggested we meet again in the morning. I agreed, but would not consent to a place for a meeting."

"Why not?"

"Because I didn't trust him. That's why not. I

*April 10, 1963

told him I would telephone him between nine o'clock and nine thirty, and give him a rendezvous of my own choosing. He brought up the question of trust himself. He said we had to trust each other completely. I didn't say anything.

"I had a really good night's sleep. One sleeps well with all that dough. Also, I had an idea that this morning Troit was going to give me the plan at last. If you are prepared to pass along twenty-seven grand, someone, somewhere has to be serious. Therefore a detailed plan had either been prepared, or was being prepared. The plan was not up to me to make. I was the mechanic. The mechanic does not take any part in drawing up the plan. He drops into the plan as prepared, pulls the trigger, and drops out again. There is no other way to do it. The assassin usually requires that he be filled in on the detailed plans up to and including that point where the execution takes place."

"What if you don't like the plan as it is presented to you?"

"You refuse to do it. There is no other way. I don't want to get myself killed any more than the next man. In this case, the assassin would be the target for instant reprisal by the Secret Service. I would have to guard against the counterattack that would almost certainly follow my pulling the trigger, unless the plan provided for shielding. After all, the Secret Service men have their job to do, and they, too, are expert marksmen.

"Troit was not an amateur. I knew that in Guatemala before the Bay of Pigs. I knew it in Haiti, and I knew it then. He was waiting for orders himself, waiting for the plan, and I had a feeling he would present it for my approval today. I started out for Troit's hotel. He was expecting me to telephone him between nine o'clock and nine-thirty. I decided just to appear and knock on his door, and then talk business in his room. At approximately twenty after nine I did just that. He opened the door, and did not seem surprised at seeing me . . ."

McDonald, "A professional reaction. He was probably expecting you to do what you did."

"I was now convinced Troit knew the tricks, and it was at that moment that I mentally committed myself to doing the job to the best of my ability. Until then I had been holding out.

"The day was very hot. The sun was bright, and the glare almost intolerable. It seemed totally unreal to be talking about plans for killing the President of the United States in that clean sunlight."

"If it were a movie you would probably be doing it around a swimming pool in the Bahamas."

"As a matter of fact, I felt better when Troit pulled the heavy drapes and turned the lamps on. That was more appropriate to dirty doings. Now he was calm, decisive, and also deadly. I thought to myself, 'I'm glad he's not pointing a gun at me.'

"He opened the conversation by telling me flatly that within the next fifteen minutes he would give me enough information concerning the attack plan that I would be irrevocably committed to my part of the job. There could be no backing out. They were planning to kill the most powerful man in the world. They would not hesitate to kill anyone who stood in the way, anyone who knew too much. I said I wasn't going to make any Goddamn commitment until I had heard the plan. If I didn't like it, if I thought it was going to get me killed too, he could take the whole thing to some other jackass."

"How did he take that?"

"He met me somewhere in the middle. He would

155

outline the plan. It would lend itself to change so that it would meet with my approval. Then it would be mandatory.

"I must point out that these are dangerous times in assassination negotiations. Once the plans were divulged I could not leave the room without total commitment on my part. If I could not accept the planning, and no alternate arrangements could be agreed on, when I left that room, Troit would have to be a dead man. So the lines were drawn. There was no doubt in my mind but that Troit had arrived at the same conclusion. If we could not agree, I was sure he planned something pretty final for me. Although there were only two of us, I was the loner, while he represented a group of enormous wealth and power. Hell, my own death warrant was being signed right there and then, so what the hell.

"Troit talked rapidly, like somebody running through a minefield to get out of it faster. I got the impression that he was so word-perfect in what he was telling me that he was doing the whole thing from memory.

"He began by saying that the time and location had not yet been firmed up. Before I had time to say 'shit,' he held up his hand, and said that, regardless of place or time, the following plan would be adhered to.

"First they had picked the fall guy, the patsy, a natural dupe to play the vitally important role of 'cover' and 'target'. I will explain these two terms. The assassin, the real assassin, me, must be assured that at the very instant of firing and immediately thereafter, some sort of protective covering device is available. A standard type of cover is found in some sort of distracting circumstance . . ."

156

"Like a pickpocket who has an accomplice bump into the victim at the moment of snatch."

"Exactly. *Exactly.* In this case, Troit told me his 'friend' would actually fire several shots from a rifle, aiming the gun close to the President. He said this man had no knowledge of the assassination plot, but would believe that he was in the pay of the CIA. He was firing the shots only to demonstrate to the President how vulnerable he was when he was not using his protective equipment, or paying no attention to the instructions of the Secret Service. The friend would actually be firing cover for me. That is to say, I would wait for his shots, fire immediately under them, and provided I fired quickly enough, no one would really hear my shots.

"But it was the next part of the plan that really proved its cleverness. Troit stated that the man who would fire the shots had recently returned from the Soviet Union with a Russian wife. He had been a defector. He was something of a psychopath. His entire background made him the natural person to become a target. The target in this context is the person in the plan who draws the return or protective fire from the Secret Service. If this person is killed, the assassination is usually considered solved, the book closed. But Troit's plot was even more devious than that. Listen carefully.

"The target would be killed. By me. The man firing shots near the President would believe —because he was told—that the Secret Service personnel were in on the arrangement, and would not try to kill him in retaliation. Therefore, after the warning shots, he would be in no particular hurry to disappear. It would be natural to wait briefly to see what happened.

"The Secret Service, of course, had no idea of the plot. They would believe the shots represented an unsuccessful attempt at assassination, and return the fire. Under cover of their fire, I was to swing my rifle onto the target and kill him. After all, they were reacting against something that had just happened. They would be in confusion, and could miss. I, on the other hand, would know exactly where he was, and draw my bead on him in cold blood. Once more, this confirmed my conviction that Troit had already picked the exact spot where the President would be killed. His plan suggested a detailed knowledge of at least two places of concealment, one for me and one for the patsy. You just don't put two people with rifles on either side of an open street. Troit had to have some location that would fit his plan.

" 'When the patsy falls dead,' Troit told me, 'the Secret Service will get the credit for killing him,' and the case would be cleared. The man's background would support the story that he was a Soviet agent, or at least a person with close ties to the International Communist movement. Troit stated that their plan included planting a bullet from this man's rifle somewhere on the scene of the assassination in order to tie his gun, not mine, to the case."

McDonald commented almost to himself, "This would account for the undamaged, pristine bullet found on the stretcher that carried Governor Connally to the hospital."

Saul went on. "I would be firing a bullet that disintegrates on contact, so there would really be no sign of a second weapon.

"The plan was as close to perfection as anything I had ever heard. The fall guy's background was

158

simply too good to be true, so good that for quite a while I didn't believe it. The plan had all the proper circumstances for the execution, and at the same time provided the authorities with the solution. It did not provide for the one human error that nearly fucked the whole thing up."

"Which was?" McDonald was instantly alert.

"I'll come to that. I now knew there were powerful interests behind Troit. I was not interested. The less I knew, the better my future health.

"Though the total plan looked good and seemed geared to smooth execution, there were several questions: the when, the where, the time. Before I could make detailed plans for my own end of the operation, I would have to have the answers. If I was to kill the President, I had to know where to go. Troit told me these answers were not yet available. As soon as they were, he would pass along the information.

"I then told Troit that I had my own operating rules. And one of them was inflexible—that I get a chance to see and study my targets before the day of execution. This rule was to protect myself and my client. I did not want to take a chance on hitting the wrong person. Hell, the President might have a double. Examining a picture was not good enough. I had to see him, more than once, and, most importantly, for periods long enough to make him and his natural movements familiar to me. The President was known to have a bad back. Did it, for example, make him limp slightly, or slouch? I had seen him on several occasions outside the United States. I felt generally I was well enough acquainted with him that I could operate efficiently. This proved to be a mistake. I will explain that later.

159

"The man who was to be my second victim was another matter altogether. It was of the utmost importance that I keep him under observation, for several days at least. I wanted this surveillance set up outside the United States. I did not want to enter the States at all until D-Day, or as near to it as possible. I wanted nobody, including Troit, to know when I entered, or when I left. I would handle these matters alone. Troit agreed. He would arrange some pretext to get the fellow to Mexico City and set him up for me to meet him."

"Did he give the man's name?"

"Yes. At that very moment. He said his name was Harvey Oswald. He did not say 'Lee.' I told Troit I did not want to *meet* Oswald, and I definitely did not want him to meet *me*. I said, get the guy to Mexico City, and have him stay there for a few days. Point him out to me and I will tail him. Troit okayed this. He said he would make contact with me with all the necessary information. I refused to give him a contact number, or a place for him to get in touch with me. I wanted to think. I told him I would contact him every three days. If extra information cropped up, he would tell me, and I would arrange a rendezvous.

"One of the real danger spots had been passed, so I holstered the small Derringer that had been in my pocket the whole time. I have no doubt Troit was doing the same thing. As I left the room Troit said that the next *meeting,* as distinct from telephone calls, would be the last one. He placed his hand on my shoulder and squeezed it hard, sincere as hell. He said, 'Remember—no mistakes allowed.' I agreed. As it happened, there were a lot."

"You are, however, keeping the story in sequence?"

"Yes." Then Saul went on.

"The next period of waiting was probably the most trying. There is nothing worse than just wait, wait, wait. I had no opportunity to practice, or rehearse, or do a dry run. All I was sure of was my professionalism, and my dead accuracy with a rifle.

"I traveled considerably, made my contact call every third day. Each time the answer was the same—the code word was 'Sunlight.' This meant that Troit had nothing new to tell me. This pattern continued for about five months. Then some time in early September I got the word I wanted. 'Longhorn.' 'Longhorn' meant that some fresh information was available and that I was to meet Troit in three days in Guatemala; I forgot to mention I happened to be in Panama at the time. The same day I left for Guatemala. On September 10th or 11th—I believe that is the date, I don't keep notes—I met with Troit, and this was Goddamn nearly the last meeting of his career.

"At ten o'clock in the morning I arrived at his room and after he ushered me in, very friendly, I found a third person there, a woman. I would guess her to be Mexican, or of Spanish descent in some way. She was attractive in a mature sort of way, several years younger than Troit, and from what I noticed of her hair, the bags under her eyes, and the bed, I guessed she had spent the night there. Troit made no attempt to introduce her. He laughed. He said she was okay. We could speak in front of her. If I felt uncomfortable, he would send her away for breakfast. I was in a rage. I ignored him, turned to the woman and said, 'Do you know why I am here?' She seemed surprised, shrugged her shoulders and said, 'Well, it has something to do with the United States.'

"I felt as if I had been punched in the nose. I told you earlier I have learned to trust my intuition, my extrasensory perception. I had a feeling that the woman, at least up to now, had no idea of what Troit and I were meeting about, but the indiscretion was crazy. My life was at stake. There flashed through my mind the idea of killing him and the woman on the spot. He had committed such a pointless, stupid error. It was incomprehensible. I kept my voice calm and told him I preferred to speak alone. He spoke to her in Spanish. She adjusted her hair briefly in front of the mirror, and left the room.

"I turned, swung my hand and caught him on the side of his face with the butt of my Derringer. He hit the floor with a thud, and I kicked him in the face. I grabbed his gray hair and bent his head back. He stared at me, only partly conscious, not uttering a sound. Believe me, my friend, when I tell you the next ten seconds sealed the fate of the President of the United States of America.

"I let his hair go, and his head lolled forward. Blood streamed from the side of his face, and his mouth. One eye was swollen shut, from where I put the boot in. He staggered to his feet. He had considerable difficulty in speaking, after what I had done to him.

"What he said was, 'Sit down.' His handkerchief held to the side of his face, he said he had set the place of the assassination. I was carefully studying his face, saying nothing. There was some fear in his one operative eye, some acknowledgment of

162

his ridiculous mistake. I think he realized he was alive only as a result of a split-second decision on my part not to kill him.

"I kept thinking that he must have introduced the woman into the picture for a reason. He was too professional to make such a stupid move. I must tell you I never found out what the reason was. I never saw her again. I never met Troit again. The last few minutes had established a wall between us—of fear, and also respect. The incident was never referred to, but it has preyed on my mind. I do not like unanswered questions . . .*

"Troit told me that the assassination was planned to take place in Dallas, Texas, in November—sometime between Monday the eighteenth and Friday the twenty-second. It was being arranged for the President to speak in that city. He would be riding in a motorcade. There would be no cover on his car, so he would be exposed to my rifle.

"I asked if he could give me the route of the President's caravan, and to have indicated on the route map the exact location where Harvey Oswald would fire the cover shots, and where I would kill him after I had killed the President. He gave me a certain location where, any time after the 15th of November, I could pick up that information. It would be drawn on a map and would be

___

*McDonald says, "I believe that even now this incident was Saul's greatest source of anxiety. The scene is so irrelevant, so stupid, and leaves such a loose end that it could not be invented. Anyone who was creating a story out of imagination would never insert an incident of this kind. It is irrelevant, nonsensical, and totally out of context with the entire central theme of Saul's story. It is one of the proofs of Saul's story. There is only one explanation: it happened. And Saul, like a camera, recorded it. As much as anything it reinforced my belief in the Saul story. I, too, don't like unanswered questions."

in a box at a postal station close to, but not in, Dallas.

"I asked about an alternate plan in case it rained, or for some other reason, President Kennedy was covered either with a hardtop automobile or his famous bullet-proof bubble. Troit told me the possibility had been considered. I was simply to leave. Plans would be rearranged.

"One final, highly important detail had to be completed, the payment of the second twenty-five thousand dollars. I had designated a bank, changing my mind, selecting Haiti. I gave Troit a name. The money was to remain in the bank for sixty days. If I did not withdraw it in that period of time, Troit would know something had happened to me, and he could withdraw the money himself. Troit agreed, and the President became a dead man.

"Several days after this final meeting, I had a sudden panic. We had not made the arrangements for me to observe Harvey Oswald who would be firing the cover shots. As you recall, the plan would only be completed successfully when I turned my weapon on him, and destroyed him in a way that would give the credit to the Secret Service. I contacted Troit and reminded him.

"He said, 'Christ!' and agreed. He stated to me he would have Oswald in Mexico City on the following dates, September 26th to October 3rd. Oswald would call on both the Cuban Consul and the Soviet Consul. Troit furnished me with the name of the hotel where Harvey Oswald would be staying. The question of how I would identify Oswald in Mexico City was not discussed, but it really presented no problem so far as I was concerned."

"Why not? Did you have a photograph?"

"No, I have a contact in the Soviet Embassy who would do the job for me."

McDonald, astounded: "You *what!?*"

Saul, "Leave it as I say it. I am not going to blow my contacts to please your curiosity. On the designated day, Mr. Oswald did show up in Mexico City. He was fingered to me. Let me tell you, after tailing the guy for three days, my faith in the overall plan was practically in shreds. I knew Oswald was a psychopath, but not to that extent. For example, on at least five occasions I sat very close to him in restaurants and cafeterias. He was always alone at mealtime, and he talked audibly to himself, all the time. His snatches of conversation were not rational. He seemed obsessed with 'Marina'—I know now, of course, that that was his Russian wife—and kept saying the words 'shining hero', and giggling to himself.

"He was also extremely nervous. He spent hours walking, aimlessly . . ."

"Did you ever see him with another person?"

"Only once."

"With whom?"

Saul hesitated, and McDonald expected a reply like, "None of your business." Saul then said, "A man at the Cuban Embassy. They left the Embassy building together. Oswald had been inside for an hour or more. They walked several blocks, and the Cuban seemed to be trying to explain something to Oswald, who kept nodding, thoughtfully. They finally halted at an intersection, and stood and talked for about ten minutes. I got close enough to get the gist. They talked in English. Oswald was trying to get a visa into Cuba.

"Another funny thing about Oswald—he carried what appeared to be an official identification

165

of some sort. It was not a passport. It appeared to be bound in a small black case. He carried it in his right-hand pants pocket, and while he was by himself, he would often take it out and look at it. On one occasion I got close enough to give it a quick glimpse. I could not read it. It had a photograph, and a small blue circular seal. I am not even sure the photograph was of Oswald. He would take this document out of his pocket every ten or fifteen minutes when seated and study it. It seemed somehow to reassure him. Perhaps it was a phony CIA identity card."

"By the description, it is more than possible. But I doubt it. It would have been found on him."

Saul went on. "Oswald lived cheaply. He didn't seem interested in food or drink—or women. He went to bed early. He would have been, in my opinion, a pathetic and lonely guy except for the fact that he was talking himself into the history books."

Part II
The Kill

"In November, 1963, I left for the United States. I will not mention where or how I crossed the border. But on the evening of the 20th I was installed in Dallas . . ."*

"I took a room in a small, pleasant hotel, and stayed there. I had no intention of exposing myself more than I had to. The city would soon be crawling with CIA, FBI, and Secret Service, and I had to reduce the possibility of recognition to a minimum, both before and after the assassination.

"On the morning of the 21st, I asked the bell captain at the hotel if he could send a messenger to pick up a package for me at a certain location outside Dallas. The hotel did have a messenger service, and arrangements were made for the envelope to be picked up and delivered to my room. If the contents were those promised by Troit, they would show the route of the President's motorcade through Dallas, and the window in which I could spot and nail Harvey

---

*Hugh McDonald comments: "As a professional assassin with an international clientèle, Saul has to master the art of crossing borders illegally, so that no record is kept. False passports are the easiest method."

Oswald (I still didn't know he had the name of Lee as well. I thought of him as 'Harvey').

"Don't think I wasn't nervous. This was the biggest assignment of my life. I am not Superman, only a guy who does a certain job professionally and well. I no longer had Troit to turn to. I had my own arrangements to firm up. From the moment I got the program, I was on my own. I had to make my own plans, take my own sights. And we were down to a matter of days before the President of the United States was to be killed.

"At eleven o'clock on the morning of the 21st, the package was delivered to me. It gave me all the information I needed. There was a map of the general area, cut from some sort of brochure, showing the streets around the Plaza. There were bus and train and airline schedules—and sort of a little booklet telling all about the city of Dallas. The important stuff was on two pieces of plain paper—a hand-drawn map showing just where the President's motorcade would come into the area and how it would proceed. There was a time schedule broken down to minutes and seconds showing where the President's car would be, and exactly when.

"As it happened, they were a little off with the times. Something must have held it up somewhere along the line. But it wasn't enough to make all that much difference.

"The hit day was November 22nd—late morning.

"On the afternoon of the 21st, I walked to the area of the Dealey Plaza."

"What were you wearing?"

"I don't remember. Probably something like I have on. No . . . it wasn't cold. I had on an open shirt and a light sweater. I was carrying a newspaper in case there was a place where I could sit down and pretend to read it while I cased the situation.

"I enjoyed the walk. Dealey Plaza is a pleasant sort of place. There were plenty of people around—coming and going, and some just hanging around like I was. Nobody paid any attention. I sat down on the grass for a while and then sort of walked around. All in all, I spent about an hour and a half orienting myself, casing the place from every angle.

"I located the sixth floor window of the building where Oswald would be stationed. This arrangement, incidentally, was strictly tentative. The instructions I had received in the envelope stated that Oswald would fire from that window only if there were no change in plan. There is always the risk of something going wrong with a nut like Oswald. In one way Oswald was an inspired choice, but in another way he was so crazy he could fuck up the whole thing. Maybe he couldn't get the window open—or maybe go to the wrong window. This, in fact had been anticipated. Oswald had been instructed to stand at the chosen window for several minutes before the President's motorcade appeared. He had been told that the Secret Service wanted to be absolutely sure where he was and that he was doing what he had been told. They told him they would recognize him because they had photographs of him. So through the scope of my own rifle it would not be difficult for me to scan each window, and locate him—if he made some mistake—because if he didn't show at all the whole deal was off.

"As soon as I had the geography of the area

down cold so I could walk it in my sleep, I located the building from which I would fire. It was across the street from the building Oswald would be in. The room I selected would give me a clear field of fire both on the President's motorcade and to the window where Oswald would be shooting.

"Then I had some disturbing thoughts. They told me Oswald was the patsy. But what if they told Oswald *I* was the patsy? Maybe he was a crack shot—and not just a nut. If I could see him through my scope, then he could see *me*. It wouldn't be the first time it's happened that way. You have to watch your ass every time—because nobody else will. I had to figure some way around that one.

"As it turned out, I did my worrying for nothing. I got my shots off—but not quite like I was supposed to.

"You know, it's a funny damn thing. I have read just about everything there is to read about the assassination, about all the accounts of what happened, all the theories. The only way I can figure it is that the people charged with finding out what happened did one of two things, or maybe both. They either were badly misled, or they deliberately withheld the true facts. Either way, it was fucked up pretty good.

"Take the bullets; what they put out as gospel makes no sense whatever, when you look at it. From where he was, Oswald could not possibly have fired them. True, the shots did indeed come from the rear of the car. I fired them. There were no shots fired from the so-called grassy knoll. There were no shots fired from in front of the car. It seems to me the photographs proved all that.

170

From what I read, half the people on the scene must have had a camera."

"Why didn't your gun attract attention?" Mc-Donald asked.

Saul: "I'll tell you why in a minute. Five shots were fired in all. Oswald fired three times. I fired twice. Just listen to me, and I will give you the sequence of the shots.

"As I left Dealey Plaza on the afternoon of the 21st of November, I could see no serious problem—provided my people were telling me the truth, and the chances were good that they were. Providing Harvey Oswald didn't go sour or lose his nerve. I didn't think Oswald's trigger finger would freeze. The organizers had planned for that by the dry run on General Walker. If it was going to freeze, it would freeze then. Oswald had tried it and liked it, and had done just the job he was orderd to do.

"I walked back to my hotel like a man with no worries in the world. It is incredible how human beings react. I was going to kill the President of the United States, and I felt completely relaxed. I chose a corner table in the hotel restaurant, and ate a good dinner . . ."

McDonald: "Cocktail? Wine?"

"Just one vodka and tonic. I went to my room, watched the TV and listened to the barrage of news about the President's visit the next day. I wasn't talking to *anybody*. Say no evil. See no evil. Hear no evil. Throughout the time I was in Dallas, I don't think I spoke a hundred words. Just get the messenger to pick up the envelope, and vodka and tonic, steak, rare, and French fries, or whatever.

"Just before retiring, I checked my weapon and

ammunition."

McDonald: "Which was?"

"I would be firing a European rifle with some special refinements of my own. I had mounted a very fine German-built scope. Normally I carried the scope and the rifle broken down in an instrument case, like a musical instrument case."

"How the devil could you get a thing like that through Customs?"

"Who said I went through Customs?"

"How did you conceal it . . . on the day?"

"Wait for it. I woke up after another good night's sleep, but now I was getting tense and couldn't stomach any breakfast. I decided I didn't want to be seen carrying *anything*—even a musical case. So I assembled my piece, scope and all —and loaded it fully.

"On my walk to the Dealey Plaza on the morning of the 22nd, the weapon was strapped to my upper body under the right armpit, the barrel extending down into the right pants leg. This was nothing new. It was a procedure I had used before when I was on assignment. I wore loose, almost baggy trousers, held up by suspenders, no belt. There was no possible way anyone could detect that I was carrying a rifle. The ammunition I used was very high velocity, not explosive, but rather, a disintegrating type. What I mean to say is, when the bullet struck any hard object, including a human skull, it shattered into fragments. I usually prefer this type of ammunition because it denies any possibility of ballistic comparison to match the weapon with the bullet. Later on I will describe what happens at the actual instant of the shooting, and how important this type of bullet becomes in the overall explanation of the assassination."

McDonald: "So here we are. November 22, 1963. Dealey Plaza, Dallas, Texas. D-Day. And approaching zero hour."

Saul: "When I look back on it, I get a few shivers. I really had so little to do with it, and knew so little about what was behind it all. All the planning had been done by others. This was *big* organization, friend, and I was only one small, key cog. Imagine the preparation that went into *everything*. How did they get him there in the first place? Who makes decisions like that? Who plans the trips? The whens and where? It would be interesting to know.

"And then the set-up of the actual hit itself, the routing of the cavalcade—to bring the President exactly into my sights—and only one minute behind schedule. To say nothing of tracking me down through half a dozen countries, selecting Oswald, sending him to Mexico. Who drew $50,000 out of what bank from what account to give me my fee with no questions asked? In my business, all this is *none* of my business. But with a hit as big as this, you can't help wondering.

"Troit, in spite of nearly screwing everything up with that Mexican hooker, had approached the problem so efficiently he had programmed my mind into believing in a plan I knew almost nothing about. And this was only the tip of the iceberg.

"From subsequent events, we see that there was a back-up plan in the event the primary plan failed. The primary plan did fail. I failed, through no fault of my own. The back-up plan worked.

"I don't say most people now believe Oswald was the assassin. I don't think they do. But they don't know who did it or how, and everybody, including that guy Garrison, in New Orleans, who tried to bring up an alternate theory, couldn't find the answers. This is not because I was so clever. It was because the backup plan succeeded in covering my errors.

"Walking from my hotel, the rifle caused me to limp. I had limped on arrival. It was a deliberate and calculated arrangement, and makes a simple and perfect disguise. I am sure that many people close to Dealey Plaza on that day, around eleven o'clock, would, if questioned, remember a man of my description walking with a very pronounced limp.

"I am not going to describe the exact location I took up, and from which I fired the shots that killed Kennedy . . .

"I will say it provided a minimum degree of security from the standpoint of interruption. However, I was banking on the excitement of the President's passing. He would only be seen for a few moments. Everybody would be concentrating on him. What I had to do would take only a few seconds, and I figured I stood little risk of being disturbed. I was able to free my weapon and fire it in less than ten seconds, which means that my total exposure to discovery would be considerably less than thirty seconds. Half a minute is a reasonable risk.

"At around eleven-forty I was near my firing position. Approximately eight minutes later, I saw Harvey Oswald for the first time. I remember how my heart started to beat. Everything up to now had been rehearsal, a game, like a movie. The sight of Oswald up there made me realize, like a blow in the eyes, it was all for real, and the President of the United States had only minutes to live. You have been in combat. You

174

know the feeling when everything becomes *now*. I could hear the sirens of the motorcade in the distance. I was standing back from my window, in shadow, and well below him. I was sure he couldn't see me. I watched him move something that looked like a box or carton. Then I saw that he had the rifle in his hands. As I watched, I saw him move back a little and sight his weapon toward the road below. It convinced me that he was the real dupe—not I. It was a great relief, I can tell you.

"I watched him intently. I thought to myself, you poor bastard, I know everything about you, yet you do not know of my existence, and I am going to kill you in a few minutes.

"The sirens were coming closer, and I knew the caravan was near. I removed my weapon, still hidden in my secluded spot. I waited until it appeared from the sound that the motorcade was almost directly outside the window. I left my hideaway and looked down just as the President's car was turning the corner. Standing away from the window, so that the muzzle of my weapon would not protrude, I picked up President Kennedy's head in my scope.

"It was not hard to identify him. He was sitting in the back seat in the right hand corner, and his wife was sitting on his left. You remember that I told you that one of my failures in this assignment was to be blamed on the fact that I had not had the chance to study the President's physical habits, the way he moved and carried himself when sitting or standing, and so on. I thought I knew him well enough. I had seen him personally in one of his tours outside the United States. This failure to understand my victim, my lack of homework I guess you would call it, led to much of the confusion and consternation which are so apparent in the studies of the assassination.

"It happened as I tell it to you now. When I first brought the President's head into my telescopic sight, he was leaning forward at an appreciable angle. My crosshairs were exactly on the back of his skull. I was waiting for Harvey Oswald to fire his first shot, and again I had a moment of panic that *he* might be waiting for *me*. He seemed to take forever, but in fact he fired on the split second. I heard the shot and almost instantaneously I squeezed the trigger. Just as my gun fired, the President straightened up from his forward position. I read later in the papers and other accounts, this sort of rocking-horse action of his was usual. It was to ease the pain in his bad back.

"As he straightened up, there came in view on my crosshairs a spot on the right shoulder and to the right of the middle of his back, and I knew that this is where the bullet would hit. It did so, drove straight through, exiting at the President's throat.* It apparently did not strike a bone, and drove on to hit Governor John Connally. I learned later that it struck the Governor's ribs, disintegrated and did severe damage to the lung cavity. Fragments of it, exiting, struck the wrist and penetrated the thigh.

"It is very interesting for me to note that in several statements, Governor Connally insisted that he was hit by the second, not the first shot. He is absolutely right. Lee Harvey Oswald fired the

---

*Earlier, Saul had said he was using a disintegrating type of bullet. His story concerning his first shot, going through the President and striking Connally is consistent with this type of ammunition. The autopsy shows that bullet penetrated the President without hitting a bone. Therefore, the bullet did not disintegrate.

first shot which struck the street behind and to the left of the President's car. I fired the second shot which hit both the President and the Governor.

"Now comes the third shot, a split second later. I realized that my first shot was low and to the right. Almost instinctively, I took the bead again on the back of the President's head, and fired. This bullet blew out the right side of his head. I was firing a semi-automatic weapon, and I am pretty sure that between my first shot and my second shot, the time spread was so minute that they could easily have sounded like one shot.

"Almost instantly following my second shot, Oswald fired again. This shot struck the right hand curb of the street. I saw it hit the ground.

"Now came the moment when I had to hit Oswald, timing my shot to the fusillade I expected from the Secret Service agents. I swung my rifle at him and took a beautiful, perfect bead on his left chest, right over his heart. At that instant he fired his third and last shot. I did not see where it struck. I was too busy. Oswald lowered his rifle and remained for several seconds standing at the window, as Troit had told me he would. I waited for the return fire from the Secret Service officers clustered over the President. All I could think of was, Fire, you dumb bastards!

"Nothing. I sweated. The seconds were passing. I took the risk of taking my eyes off Oswald to see what the hell the bodyguards were doing. No shots were ever fired. I could not complete the final and vital part of my contract without exposing my position. I was furious. I lowered my rifle, put it back inside my clothes.

"It is, to this day, inconceivable to me that a well-armed screen around the President of the United States, all crack shots, failed to return one shot at a man in full view, who had just fired not one, not two, but three shots at the President's car.

"This was the flaw that upset the assassination plan. Had just one of the officers fired at Oswald, I would have killed him. He was so perfectly in my sights, it was, in its own way, a crime not to kill him . . ."*

Saul: "The assassination would have been clean, solved on the spot. I would have killed Oswald, and he would have tumbled from the window. The Secret Service would have been covered with glory. A medal for somebody. I don't know why they didn't fire. I seemed to have him in my crosshairs for an eternity.

"Then he disappeared from the window. I watched the entrance to the building from which Oswald fired the shots. I saw the poor bastard come out and turn to the left. He crossed the street at the intersection, and out of my view. That is the last I saw of him. I limped out of the building, and in two hours was out of the United States."

That was the end of Saul's conversation with Hugh McDonald.

Again—where could he take his information? Who would listen?

---

*McDonald comments, "In my own way, too, I can't resist this guy's professionalism. Still furious at missing with the first shot, furious at the inefficiency of the Secret Service."

Artist's rendition of Saul's firing position as related to Oswald's sixth story position. Saul fired from a second floor window of the building on the far right of the picture, the County Records Building.

(Illustration by Michael Brian)

Appendix I
The Warren Report

Hugh McDonald needed more proof of the integrity of Saul's statement. He had learned over the years that nothing fascinates a certain kind of psychopath more than false confession to a *cause célèbre*. McDonald felt Saul was telling the truth because Saul told almost exactly the same story Herman Kimsey had told.

Where to go next?

Easy answer: the Warren Report.

McDonald would turn the Warren Report inside out. Whereas the Report emphasized everything that proved Oswald's guilt, McDonald would concentrate exclusively on the sections of the report that dealt with the possibility of conspiracy. In other words, Lee Harvey Oswald would be eliminated in his study as the direct killer of the President.

First he studied the vital evidence of "the Miracle Bullet" that is Commission Exhibit No. 399. Drs. Dolce and Light, both recognized ballistics experts from the Army wounds ballistics branch, Edgewood Arsenal, concluded positively that bullet 399 would not support the Commission's single-bullet conclusion, because it could not have passed through Governor Connally's body without having suffered more distortion.

Dr. Olivier, another wound ballistics expert, withheld his conclusion until further tests had been conducted by firing a similar bullet into the wrist of a cadaver. The test validated Drs. Light and Dolce's opinion. The bullet emerged from the cadaver's wrist (after closely simulating Governor Connally's wrist injury) with a flattened nose.

FBI and other ballistic experts *did* identify the nearly pristine bullet, found at Parkland Hospital, as having been fired from Oswald's rifle. There is no doubt of this point. But no ballistic expert anywhere or at anytime testified that the Parkland Hospital bullet, CE No. 399, did or could have caused all the damage subscribed to it by the Commission's single bullet theory.

McDonald continues: "Remember Saul's statement. Long before the Warren Commission even existed he had been told that there was a possibility that such a bullet would be planted to tie in Oswald's rifle positively to the shooting. It therefore appears that the mere existence of CE No. 399 tends to prove the accuracy of Saul's statement and the presence of a conspiracy."

Third: The Warren Commission report totally supports Saul's statement in its contention that all of the shots came from the rear of the President's car. Many of the dissidents, and most recently certain commenters on the Zapruder film, try to prove their point that there had to be someone firing from in front of the car because of the action of the President's head. That is, it's snapping backwards almost instantaneously on bullet impact. Those not familiar with the reaction of a target such as the human skull to the impact of a speeding bullet are frequently led to believe that the reaction as shown in the film testifies to the fact that the impact had to come from in front.

"This is not so.

"A high velocity rifle bullet penetrates with such speed that there would not necessarily be movement in any direction. There would be a reaction similar to that of firing through a half open door. The door would be penetrated but would not move much.

"In the case of the skull, when the bullet penetrates, it travels through a very small and absolutely air-tight vault. Tremendous pressure is built up in front of it. The bullet on contact loses shape, so that when it exits through the opposite side of the skull, the combination of pressure and the misshapen slug creates a tremendous explosion. The force of the explosion forces the skull *backwards* in reaction to the opposite force. The head moves directly towards the spot from which the bullet was fired. It is the lack of understanding of these forces that has created much of the confusion about the direction from which the bullet was fired.

"The Warren Report insists, and the wounds ballistics experts all agree, that all of the shots that struck the President came from the rear. How does this information square with Saul's story given to Kimsey long before the Warren Report was published? Saul had no way of knowing that there would be a Zapruder film. He had no way of knowing that there would be so much speculation concerning the direction from which the shots were fired.

"He was simply telling the truth.

"In his statement he did comment on the confu-

183

sion about the direction of the shots, and he was pleased to be able to clear it up. It seems then that in those areas where the experts agree with the conclusions of the Warren Commission, that their opinions support Saul's story completely.

"Finally, the Warren Commission states that they were absolutely unable to find any motive for Oswald to kill President Kennedy. This confirms Saul's statement that Oswald had no motive or desire to kill the President. He, in fact, thought he was serving the best interests of the Chief Executive.

"Until one reads Saul's testimony, there is also the confusion about Oswald's trip to Mexico shortly before the assassination. Why did he make the trip? And why was he, even then, under CIA surveillance?* Oswald did not have much money, so it could not have been a pleasure trip. The trip had to have something to do with the President. Saul tells the story. Compare his account with that of the Warren Report: testimony is quoted of someone who '. . . sat opposite him in a Mexico City restaurant because the place was full. They did not speak.'

"The Report states Oswald took a bus at the terminal of Flecha Roga bus line, Calle Heroes Ferrocarrileros 45. That's all. No hint of relevance. It gives this magnificent sequence of uninformation, even anti-information: it concerns one Albert Osborne, described as 'an elderly itinerant preacher' whom 'two Australian girls' said sat next to Oswald on the bus to Mexico City. But Mr. Osborne 'denied it'; however, 'Osborne's responses to

---

The New York Times recently reported on an unusual public statement by the CIA regarding Lee Harvey Oswald's visit to Mexico between late September and early October, 1963.

Federal investigators on matters unrelated to Oswald have proved inconsistent and unreliable' so 'the Commission has attached no credence to his denial'. However 'to the other passengers on the bus it appeared that Osborne and Oswald had never met, and extensive investigation revealed no more Oswald-Osborne meetings, and so after investigation of his [Osborne's] background and activities, the Commission found no basis for suspecting him in any involvement in the assassination . . .''

"That is not all. The Warren Report states, 'Investigation of the hotel at which Oswald stayed has failed to uncover any evidence that the hotel is unusual in any way that could relate to Oswald's visit.'

"This meaningless post-murder drivel goes on and on for page after page. Yet, just before the murder, the FBI and CIA were covering every move that Oswald was making . . . and the President was not yet dead."

McDonald comments: "The material we have just gone over seems somehow to relieve me of total responsibility in publishing Saul's story and putting my life-long reputation on the line by saying I believe the man told me the truth. There are some other points brought to light by the Chief Justice himself that seem to secure Saul's story in a far better way than anything I could say. It is extraordinary how the truth comes out in the end. Look at Nixon and Watergate. Once the ball starts rolling it doesn't stop until it comes to rest."

Appendix 2
The Back-up

Hugh McDonald believes:

The back-up link in the plot to assassinate President Kennedy was, of necessity, the plot to kill Oswald, should he not be killed first by the Secret Service, firing from the street below, or by Saul, under cover of their shots.

At least two key men would have to be selected, blinkered like the rest from the larger scheme, to do the killing. At the same time, insiders would have to select the back-up men, and they would have to be men on the spot.

The original premise was that it was inconceivable anyone could assassinate a President of the United States, and not be gunned down instantly by the protective screen of the Secret Service, armed, trained, carefully selected, expert men. Hence the stipulated plan for Saul: his final shot mingling with those of the Secret Service to kill Oswald in the window of the Book Depository building. With this successfully achieved, the back-up men could go home and sleep in peace.

It wasn't.

There had to be *two* key men: the first (the "outside" man) to track and kill Oswald in the seemingly remote eventuality that he escaped entirely undetected, the second (the "inside" man) to eliminate Oswald if he were to be caught alive and taken into custody.

The "outside man" is so far unknown. He obviously failed.

The "inside man" . . .

The same organizers who so brilliantly selected Saul and Lee Harvey Oswald for their prospective roles, picked Jack Ruby. Jack Ruby had access to the police department, vitally important. The Dallas police force was probably an unknown factor, so it would be too risky to try to recruit a back-up man from the force itself.

Whether or not Lee Harvey Oswald was convinced that his shots—aimed to miss—had "killed" the President, he panicked. His state of mind can barely be dreamed of. He had fired, and as he fired, he saw the President's skull explode in a pink mist. McDonald agrees with the Warren Report on what happened then. Oswald went to his room, and, probably, armed himself with a revolver. He probably did not know why. He may have wanted, dizzily, to kill himself, or kill the men who had made him the fall guy in a Presidential assassination. He was in a state of paralyzed shock, with no way out. He rushed out of his room, down the street. Patrolman Tippitt saw a man in a state of uncontrollable emotion, stopped his patrol car to question him. The irony was that the entire world was stunned at that moment, Tippitt, too. Had Oswald been able to cling to the shreds of rationality, he could have screamed, "The President has been shot!" Instead, he pulled out his gun and shot Tippitt dead.

It was high noon. He needed the dark to pull together his crazed mind. He saw a movie theater. He threw money at the ticket window and went inside. It was the last free action of his life. Some-one, upon seeing a half-crazy man rush into the theater, had telephoned the police. Oswald, still frightened out of his wits, saw the picture stop, the house lights go on, and a group of policemen and detectives closing in on him from every door.

He pulled out his gun, pointed it at the police captain and screamed, "This is the end!" The police probably believed it. But the gun misfired. The man who, in official history, goes down as the greatest marksman since William Tell blew an apple off his son's head with an arrow, was over-powered and taken into custody. He had lost his last wish. He must certainly have hoped he would be cut down by police bullets and be put out of his misery.

He had, in an hour, escaped death three times: once from Saul, as Saul and his bosses intended; once from the "outside man;" and once from the police, as he, Oswald, hoped. Perhaps four times, if Patrolman Tippitt had been quicker on the draw. And so, in a story which builds irony upon irony upon irony, his arrest was his death war-rent. He *had* to be killed, and as quickly as possi-ble. He *must not* have time to tell his true role in the conspiracy. The last back-up plan went into effect.

Jack Ruby, a wretch of a man with hoodlum connections, sought to keep his nose clean by kiss-ing the ass of the police force. His world was the world of sleazy nightclubs and strippers, with all the concomitants of prostitution, protection, pay-offs to the right guys, free drinks and babes, the uneasy Jewish-Sicilian freemasonry of the Mafia, the hustling of a buck, the beating of girls who won't play, and the "hi-pal" bonhomie.

Ruby, McDonald continues, was undoubtedly paid a substantial sum of money for his back-up role. He was assured at the same time that it *was* a back-up, and he would never have to earn it. Which was something of a pity, he was told, because his role would make him an American hero. The cops knew him, and called him "Jack." The logic of this is, with the hindsight of time, overwhelming. Who would punish a man for killing Sirhan Sirhan immediately after the death of Bobby Kennedy, or Ray, the killer of Martin Luther King, or Bremer, the attempted assassin of Wallace?

Jack Ruby died in prison of cancer. He made his place in history, which is what he wanted. In his own imagination at least, he was "the Avenger."

About Oswald as killer, according to the Warren Report, McDonald has some questions:

"If Oswald wanted a place in history, why didn't he proclaim his act instead of denying it repeatedly—and then refuse to talk to police at all?

"If he did in fact have a compulsion to be caught, why did he run away? If he did want to run away, why did he head for his room, instead of for the nearest route out town? (He had with him only $13.87 for get-away money, having left Marina $170.00)."

Dr, William Offenkrantz, of the University of Chicago, has one easy answer: "Criminals who unconsciously arrange for their own capture are not rare. A more bizarre possibility is that by refusing to talk, he [Oswald] was not just waiting for a lawyer, but perhaps enjoying the sadistic pleasure of rendering the police impotent and help-less."

"To me," McDonald says, "none of Oswald's ac-tions are those of a man who has knowingly just committed a murder. They are the actions of a man totally confused—misled, betrayed, irra-tional, perhaps—but not guilty of the crime he is supposed to have committed."

Appendix 3
The Conspiracy

As Hugh McDonald pointed out earlier, the Warren Commission turned police procedure upside down. Instead of starting with the assassination of President Kennedy and tracking down the murderer, they started with Lee Harvey Oswald and backtracked him to the assassination, dismissing any evidence which might prove, within reasonable doubt, that he might not have done it.

McDonald declares that three elements are taken into account when detectives are called to a murder:

The first element to seek is *motive*. Why was the victim killed?

The second element is *capacity*. When motive and capacity have been established, the next check is on *opportunity*.

There is no such thing as a statue of limitations on murder. Cases remain open until the uncaught murderer is presumed too old to be still surviving. The case of Jack the Ripper remained on the files of Scotland Yard until after the Second World War.

When detectives meet for their daily morning conference, after they have discussed pending cases, they will pull some half-forgotten case out of their files, and simply talk about it. It often happens that something clicks and someone has a thought about it; some point that has always been there, under their nose which went unnoticed. Or, just as often, some case that happened afterwards gives a fresh lead back to the old case.

Plenty of competent detectives were available at the time the President was assassinated. In fact, every detective in America would have given his mother to the Arabs for a chance to sink his teeth into the case. But those employed were given only subordinate roles. The Warren Commission gave the orders, and it was simply not qualified to do so. To form a Commission of reluctant and unhappy civilians to investigate a stupendous murder, and not include on the panel one single expert police interrogator, beggars belief. And once the Report was issued, the Commission dissolved itself. There was no door to knock on with fresh evidence. There were no detectives to kick the case around for fresh evidence, or maybe just a brainwave.

There was nowhere to go, and no way to go about it.

Investigators, from the competent to the kooks, have been frustrated in their efforts to examine the books. Kennedy has been dead now for twelve years, but McDonald finds buck-passing in Washington still so pervasive that he cannot escape suspicion of a continued and officially-backed cover-up.

The murder of a President, or any political figure, McDonald argues, is, by definition, a political murder, and he gives four motives for political assassination:

The first is the killing by the screwball. The victim is condemned to death for no reason other than that he holds political office. His glamor helps to seal his doom.

The second motive is revenge for wrongs, real or imagined, against individuals, or groups with grievances.

The third motive, perhaps the most common, is when the holder of political office is assassinated because his enemies know of no other way to get rid of him, when the democratic process has broken down. Julius Caesar, Patrice Lumumba, Sheik Mujib of Bangladesh, Rafael Trujillo; the list is endless. This category removes one leader usually in order to be replaced by a group. The same category eliminated politicians considered a threat to the Establishment: Trotsky by Stalin: Pin Yang by Mao Tse Tung; and the legally-approved assassination of Beria by Khrushchev, Malenkov and Bulganin.

The fourth motive, McDonald argues, is the most sinister, and the most frightening. This is the killing of a holder of political office because his political policies are against the interests of powerful groups, both multi-national and national. The most recent, and blatant, is the assassination in 1973 of Dr. Salvador Allende of Chile.

The Warren Commission considered only the first three categories. The fourth was never even discussed. Lee Harvey Oswald, psychopath, fitted perfectly into the first. Lee Harvey Oswald, aggrieved underdog, disgruntled Marine, fitted the second. Oswald, the possible Communist agent, could fit with comfort into the third. Because the fourth category never came into consideration, it was never discussed how ideally he slotted in as the perfect fall-guy in a conspiracy to get rid of a President too rich to influence and too glamorous to defeat.

"And above all—
"Why didn't the Warren Commission ask these questions?"

Appendix 4
Why Did Saul Talk?

As with every stupendous incident in history, each solution creates more problems. Saul's story clears some waters only to muddy others. The question of who organized, engineered and financed the killing is speculated upon elsewhere. The human question hanging on this whole history is, why on earth did Saul tell Herman Kimsey the story in the first place? What was the motivating factor? He was home free, with his money.

Great oaks from little acorns grow, and history is written in a grain of sand, and so on in endless clichés, but cliché is only a lazy formula for truth. If the Bay of Pigs had not happened, Kimsey would not have known. Kimsey, hired by Hugh McDonald, would not have told McDonald. McDonald would not have become so obsessed by his responsibility to Goldwater. McDonald, hired to investigate Vozrozdenya, would not have known of Saul's existence.

Everything turns on the missing link. Why did Saul spill the beans to Herman Kimsey?

Hugh McDonald says, "I believe I know why Saul told the whole story to Herman Kimsey. About Kimsey first: he was a strange and lonely man, dedicated to the CIA to the point of fanaticism. If the Central Intelligence Agency wanted something, he did not give a damn how he got it. Physically he was fierce, with massive shoulders. Facially, he resembled a younger Sydney Greenstreet. Occasionally, after a mission, he would rest up in my apartment for a few days, occasions dreaded by my wife and children, simply because of his internal bitterness and loneliness, and the savageness of his views. He believed in nothing. Many people today are atheists, but Herman carried his atheism like a personal chip on the shoulder. If you suggested you believed in God, it was almost a *casus belli* —'Come and settle this outside, you sonofabitch' sort of thing.

"Kimsey's only passion was horses, and he actually ring-mastered horse shows at Madison Square Garden, wearing a tall silk hat and riding boots. He was also the best graphologist in the Central Intelligence Agency.

"I know that whatever else he did for the CIA he was the 'mentor' or 'contact man' for people the Agency wanted to place under contract for certain specific periods of time to complete specific and once-only assignments. Herman, on occasions, over the years I had known him, talked cautiously about some assignments that seemed to me to be of extraordinary sensitivity and where a man such as Saul might be used. I therefore believe that Herman was the 'mentor' or 'contact' for Saul wherever Saul worked with the Agency.

"This idea brings my original meeting with Saul into proper focus. When Saul stormed into Herman's office on that day in 1961 he was complaining to the man who was responsible for his being on the bloody beach in Cuba. If this was true, then it seems perfectly natural that Saul would go

199

back to Herman Kimsey to complain again for the botching up of the biggest job in his, Saul's, life. As at the 'Bay Of Pigs' he felt that the failure was not his fault. None of the Secret Service men fired back at Oswald, therefore there was no way Saul could complete his assignment. The only contact he had and trusted was Herman Kimsey . . . his agency mentor.

"At the time of the assassination of President Kennedy, Herman Kimsey was working for the Agency. I don't know exactly when he left them or why. I was shocked when I first heard that he was out. And more than shocked when I learned that he received no pension. Herman simply would not talk about it. I could sense disappointment in his attitude when the subject was mentioned, but he was never vindictive. He defended the Agency and everything it did.

"I have speculated that Herman Kimsey never really left the Agency. That his resignation was part of a plan to divorce his actions from the Agency, and that he was the contact man who hired Troit to set up the killing of the President. Or that he was Troit himself. I do not believe that the facts substantiate either of these approaches. First of all, if Herman was Troit, it would not have been necessary for him to search for Saul. He would have known how to contact him. Secondly, when I talked to Saul, he told me about his involvement before he saw the typed pages of Herman's account. Saul knew that I was close to Herman and he would have to reason that if Herman told me part of the story he would have revealed the entire affair. *Saul never even hinted at the possibility of Herman's involvement.*

"I think that, because of the enormity of his act,

200

Saul had to talk to *someone*. You just don't kill the President of the United States, walk away from it and then not mention it to anyone forever. I am sure that Saul was *compelled* to talk about the assassination. After the chase through Europe, I am convinced that he talked about it to several people. That would explain some of my contacts' instantaneous coupling of my query concerning Saul's whereabouts with the Kennedy assassination. Talking to *anyone* would relieve the pressure.

"All of these are possibilities. With the exception of the one tying Herman Kimsey directly to the act, I don't believe any of them fit perfectly. Like a jigsaw puzzle when you're trying to use a piece where it doesn't belong, you have to push too hard to make it fit. I get that same feeling with each of these concepts."

Appendix 5
Saul Today?

Somewhere, perhaps in Europe, or perhaps on the same soil as the reader of this book, prowls the man who was paid to kill President Kennedy—and did. Hugh McDonald does not know where he is, but he can do a lot of educated guessing. Saul moves from country to country, avoiding the United States except in extremis, but keeping in touch with his contacts in Mexico and Guatemala. In theatrical parlance, "he calls *them,* they don't call him," unless they are desperate to get a job done. He looks in and asks if anything is going.

He will spend much time in Europe. He has no wife or children, and no friends. A friend who is not curious is not a friend, and friends want to know what the friend is up to. Above all, he dares not risk a steady girl friend, and the risk of the fury that no hell hath. His sexual relationships are essentially transient.

For his hobby, he almost certainly hunts. Shooting is his life, and the shedding of blood. He is a voracious reader of newspapers, and is as well-informed as any editor. He has to know what is going on in the world, just as a banker has to know the stock market.

He goes to the movies a great deal because time hangs heavy for a professional assassin, and he is never in one place long enough to become a TV addict. Fundamentally a European, he will prefer soccer to football.

Like all rogues, rascals and adventurers throughout history, he is drawn to the Mediterranean and spends as much time there as in Central America.* But the Riviera is too stratified and cliquey. The Riviera means gossip, and the bitchier the better, and strangers are quickly noticed and commented on.

He is undoubtedly more comfortable in the more raffish and seedy resorts like Torremolinos, Malaga, Benidorm and Ibiza. Especially the Clifford Irving island of Ibiza. It is Saul's world. There, nobody has a second name, and the four forbidden words are "What do you do?" On Ibiza, there are no parties, no invitations, and the island abounds in people with secrets to hide. Saul would fall happily into the social scene and never be noticed. On Ibiza, people come, find a favorite bar, make a few bar chums, pick up girls, and then disappear for weeks, months, years, return, and are welcomed as casually and indifferently as if they had never been away. Ibiza is an island without curiosity or memory. When you are there, you are there. When you are gone, you are forgotten. For Saul: sanctuary.

He probably maintains a quiet, inexpensive room the year round in a small Left-Bank hotel in Paris, to keep his things. When he is "between engagements," his guns are stored in safety deposit boxes.

He is not always a wise or prudent man. To come into the smart, American-oriented Westbury

---

*For escape of tensions, but also for professional reasons. Marseilles and Naples are two of the most valuable markets in the world.

Hotel in Mayfair, set between Bond Street and Regent Street, without a tie, is, in itself, an act of considerable stupidity. The reception clerks and concierge would regard him disapprovingly, and the heads of the hotel guests would turn. Hugh McDonald, a conservative and correct dresser, noticed it subconsciously even at the moment of the shattering impact of confrontation.

Saul's adrenalin is such that he is probably indifferent to food. McDonald was with him long enough to decide he had recently given up smoking. There were still nicotine stains on his fingers.

Hugh McDonald does not believe that Saul will ever crack up or feel his finger freeze on the trigger. But Saul is growing older. His competition is not only younger, but the new mechanics are the product of a world which makes him progressively an amateur. These are the graduates of the more diabolical universities of the Palestine Liberation Organization, the urban guerillas of the Argentine and Uruguay, and the Provisional Irish Republican Army. Worse still, some of them, like the Japanese Red Army, do not mind dying on the job. Were Saul an Englishman, he would consider this "not cricket." What Saul would call "profession," they call "mission."

Saul's eyesight will not always be so penetrating, his reflexes so quick. Even now he prefers to sit rather than stand in the subway on a single-station trip. Inevitably, he has many failures as well as successes. His batting average, based on two adventures, the Bay of Pigs and Kennedy, is not perfect. Today the uproar over Kennedy's assassination is greater than it has ever been. Throughout his career, having taken an irrevocable fifty per cent of his commission in advance, he lives in fear of employers who, while they have accepted the risks, are justifiably furious at paying out hot and dangerous, laundered money for no result. Those who tried the job again with a different mechanic, might suggest that the mechanic might pull his next trigger on Saul. Saul, by definition and the dead-reckoning of cold reason, is a frightened man, and probably prematurely aged.

So, even if this book does not achieve McDonald's purpose and ambition, namely to have the case re-opened and he, McDonald, called to Congressional Committee to testify under oath, the law-abiding reader of the book can take a certain consolation. Crime might pay, and crime does pay, but the more tremendous the success, the deeper and hotter the Hell.

Appendix 6
Hugh McDonald Concludes...

A criminal President has resigned, accepted a pardon and still has the audacity to proclaim his innocence. Young people are so turned off by politics that they don't take the trouble to go to the polls. America, at the seat of government, is so sick that many doubt its ability to recover. Nutty kids with names like Squeakie Fromme go into the history books by pointing a 1913 revolver at an unelected President, only narrowly failing to emulate other creeps called Sirhan Sirhan, Ray and Bremer.

How much of this can be traced directly to that first deliberate outrage perpetrated against the American people, the Warren Commission Report?

The assassination of President John F. Kennedy was a tragedy. Tragedy is something we all live with. But to many the Warren Report was a sham.

In the midst of the shock, while the tears of the world were still flowing, the oddities began. President Johnson, although he could call on the finest investigative agencies of the country, chose instead to create a Commission. His first thought was to create an all-Texan commission, and so wipe clean the reputation of the state of Texas. His advisers pointed out that the idea was ludicrous, and he went along with them.

His second and final choice was a commission headed by the Chief Justice of the Supreme Court, Mr. Earl Warren, who, perhaps with Adlai Stevenson, was the most distinguished and revered living American. The Commission's sole reason for existence was to investigate and fix responsibility for the assassination of the President, and the members were counted on to come up with what they considered to be the best solution. Surely they couldn't say to hell with any facts that might upset the previously agreed status quo.

Thus the sickness began, and from that day to this it has grown through the whole fibre of American society. Trust no one. Tell the people only what is good for them to know. Conceal the truth in the clever use of words and the manipulation of facts. Cover up. Deny. Figure out the "scenario." Try for a limited "hang-out."

Joseph Kinglake, the English Victorian historian, wrote an epic nine-volume history of the Crimean War (1853-1856). He based it on the papers given him by the widow of the British commander, Lord Raglan. At the conclusion of this huge, and highly readable work, Kinglake comments —and this is in 1883:

> And now I have to state that which will not surprise my own countrymen, but which will, in the eyes of the foreigner, seem passing strange. For some years, our statesmen, our admirals and our generals, have known that the whole correspondence of the English Headquarters was in my hands; and very many of them have, from

209

time to time, conversed and corresponded with me on the business of the war. Yet I declare I do not remember that any one of these public men has ever said to me that there was anything which, for the honor of our arms, or for the credit of the nation, it would be well to keep concealed. Every man has taken it for granted that what was best for the repute of England was the truth.

We are living in a period of Kennedy uproar. The time is right to investigate the real truth, without scenarios or limited hang-outs. The time is at hand to let the politicians in Washington know that the American people are capable of handling any truth, no matter what its contents, and that those same people are fed up to the teeth in being told lies.

And it all began with the Warren Report. Many well-founded challenges have been proffered, well and clearly written, concerning the Report, to the extent that the Report itself is all but discredited today.

Is there *nobody* among our elected officials who will stand up and say, "Let's have the *facts!*"

Hugh C. McDonald
Playa del Rey
California
September, 1975

Appendix 7
Hugh McDonald's Credentials

THE
PRESIDENT
OF
THE UNITED STATES OF AMERICA

To all who shall see these presents, greeting:

Know Ye, that reposing special trust and confidence in the patriotism, valor, fidelity and abilities of ___Hugh Chisholm McDonaId___ *I do appoint him* ___Major, Military Intelligence___ *in the*

Army of the United States

such appointment to date from the ___ninth___ *day of* ___May___ *nineteen hundred and* ___fifty-two___ *He is therefore carefully and diligently to discharge the duty of the office to which he is appointed by doing and performing all manner of things thereunto belonging.*

He will enter upon active duty under this commission only when specifically ordered to such active duty by competent authority.

And I do strictly charge and require all Officers and Soldiers under his command who he shall be employed on active duty to be obedient to his orders as an officer of his grade and position. And he is to observe and follow such orders and directions, from time to time, as he shall receive from me, or the future President of the United States of America, or the General or other Superior Officers set over him, according to the rules and discipline of War.

This commission continues an appointment in the Army of the United States under the provisions of section 37, National Defense Act as amended, and is to continue in force for a period of five years from the date above specified and during the pleasure of the President of the United States, for the time being.

Done at the City of Washington, this ___ninth___ *day of* ___May___ *in the year of our Lord one thousand nine hundred and* ___fifty-two___ *and of the Independence of the United States of America the one hundred and* ___seventy-sixth___

By the President:

Major General
The Adjutant General

W.D.A.G.O. FORM No. 0130C
16 October 1948

Army of the United States

Retired Reserve

*This is to certify that
by authority of the Secretary of the Army,*

HUGH CHISHOLM McDONALD
Major Military Intelligence USAR O 804 248

*has been transferred to the Retired Reserve in recognition
of honorable service and continued interest in the defense of
our Nation, on the* twenty-third *day of* November

One Thousand Nine Hundred and fifty-six

HAROLD E. ELLIOTT

Major, AGC

DA FORM 877
1 JULY 1953

FEDERAL BUREAU OF INVESTIGATION
UNITED STATES DEPARTMENT OF JUSTICE

Issues this award thereby certifying that

Hugh Chisholm Mc Donald

Los Angeles County, California, Sheriff's Department

has completed a general course of instruction afforded by the

FBI National Academy
United States Department of Justice

at Washington in the District of Columbia for a period of twelve weeks ending this the seventh day of June in the year of our Lord one thousand nine hundred and sixty-one and by these presents he is entitled to such professional standing as a law enforcement officer as may be properly accorded by reason of the completion by him of such course of instruction

Los Angeles County Sheriff

AIRMAN AWARD CERTIFICATE

Presented to

Chief H. E. McDonald

In recognition of his distinguished accomplishments
in the field of aerial support to Law Enforcement.
His meritorious service rendered to the people of
Los Angeles County provided aid and assistance
to those in distress through contributions of his
skill as an aircraft pilot in the . . .

Sheriff's Aero Squadron

Presented on April 13, 1965.

_____
Sheriff, Los Angeles County

COUNTY OF LOS ANGELES

Hugh C. McDonald

Who — HAS SERVED WITH DISTINCTION IN ALMOST EVERY DIVISION OF THE SHERIFF'S DEPARTMENT AT VARIOUS TIMES, HOLDING POSITIONS AS CHIEF OF THE CIVIL DIVISION, AS CHIEF OF THE TECHNICAL SERVICES DIVISION, AND IS RETIRING AS CHIEF OF THE DETECTIVE DIVISION.

Who — DURING HIS TWENTY-SIX YEARS OF DEDICATED SERVICE HAS DEVELOPED MANY IMPORTANT INNOVATIONS IN THE LAW ENFORCEMENT FIELD, THE MOST NOTABLE BEING THE "IDENT-A-KIT," AS WELL AS BEING THE AUTHOR OF SEVERAL BOOKS ON SUBJECTS BOTH IN AND OUTSIDE OF THE LAW ENFORCEMENT FIELD, AND

Whose — DEVOTED SERVICE TO THE SHERIFF'S DEPARTMENT HAS MADE IT A BETTER, MORE EFFICIENT INSTRUMENTALITY OF COUNTY GOVERNMENT, A RECORD OF ENVIABLE PERFORMANCE WHICH HAS BEEN APPROPRIATELY RECOGNIZED BY BOTH HIS ASSOCIATES IN THE LAW ENFORCEMENT FIELD AND MY MEMBERS OF THE BOARD OF SUPERVISORS OF THE COUNTY OF LOS ANGELES.

JANUARY 17, 1967

WARREN M. DORN
Supervisor, Fifth District
County of Los Angeles

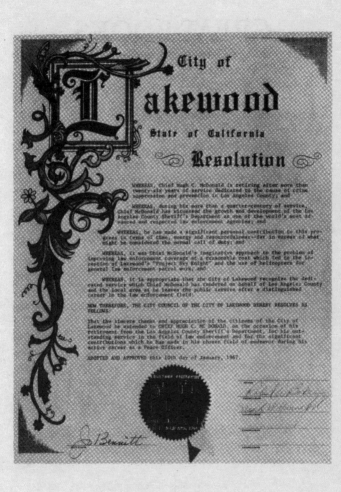

City of
Lakewood
State of California
Resolution

WHEREAS, Chief Hugh C. McDonald is retiring after more than twenty-six years of service dedicated to the cause of crime suppression and prevention in Los Angeles County; and

WHEREAS, during his more than a quarter-century of service, Chief McDonald has witnessed the growth and development of the Los Angeles County Sheriff's Department as one of the world's most advanced and respected law enforcement agencies; and

WHEREAS, he has made a significant personal contribution to this project in terms of time, energy and resourcefulness--far in excess of what might be considered the normal call of duty; and

WHEREAS, it was Chief McDonald's imaginative approach to the problem of improving law enforcement coverage at a reasonable cost which led to the inception of Lakewood's "Project Sky Knight" and the use of helicopters for general law enforcement patrol work; and

WHEREAS, it is appropriate that the City of Lakewood recognize the dedicated service which Chief McDonald has rendered on behalf of Los Angeles County and the local area as he leaves the public service after a distinguished career in the law enforcement field.

NOW THEREFORE, THE CITY COUNCIL OF THE CITY OF LAKEWOOD HEREBY RESOLVES AS FOLLOWS:

That the sincere thanks and appreciation of the citizens of the City of Lakewood be extended to CHIEF HUGH C. MC DONALD, on the occasion of his retirement from the Los Angeles County Sheriff's Department for his outstanding service in the field of law enforcement and for the significant contributions which he has made in his chosen field of endeavor during his active career as a Peace Officer.

ADOPTED AND APPROVED this 10th day of January, 1967.